The Healing

Poems By

JORDAN WELLS

Other works by Jordan Wells

LOGGED OFF: MY JOURNEY OF ESCAPING THE SOCIAL MEDIA WORLD

MIRRORS AND REFLECTIONS

Signature

The Healing

JORDAN WELLS

Scott and Scholars Press
East Orange, New Jersey 07017

Scott and Scholars Press® is a registered trademark of
Jordan Wells Publishing.

Publisher's Cataloging-in-Publication Data

Names: Wells, Jordan, author.
Title: The Healing / Jordan Wells.
Description: East Orange, NJ: Jordan Wells, 2020.
Identifiers: LCCN 2020915993 | ISBN 978-1-7355523-4-7 (Paperback)
Subjects: LCSH Poetry, American. | American poetry--21st century. | Emotions--Poetry. | African Americans--Poetry. | Love poetry, American. | BISAC POETRY / American / General | POETRY / American / African American | POETRY / Subjects & Themes / Death, Grief, Loss | POETRY / Subjects & Themes / Love & Erotica
Classification: LCC PS3623.E4698 H43 2020| DDC 811/.6--dc23

ISBN: 978-1-7355523-5-4 (eBook)

First Edition 2020

Jacket design by Jordan Wells/in collaboration
With www.thelovinglion.com

For special inquiries, please email us at scottandscholarspress@yahoo.com

Printed in the United States of America

10 9 8 7 6 5 4 3 2 1

Contents

I would like to dedicate this book to; well, you the reader. I dedicate this book to you. For it is you who found this book and decided to read it. You are the one who motivates me to create more work. May this book, in some way, give you some entertainment, some enjoyment, but most importantly, the healing.

Introduction

For some of you, we meet again. For others, this may be your first time reading any of my work. For those of you who have read my first book, "*Logged Off: My Journey of Escaping the Social Media World,*" and my second book, "Mirrors and Reflections," I say welcome back and thank you, thank you, thank you. Thank you for taking the first two journeys with me and taking one more with this book. You are amazing and I appreciate you. But yes, to the newcomers, this is my third book; third time is the charm, as some would say.

I find this to be so surreal. I remember when I was writing my first book. I was just writing the first three pages, thinking to myself, "I have such a long way to go." But I kept going, kept writing, and now here I am. You are now reading my third book, and with this book, I have a lot to say. A lot of things on my mind, that I did not reveal in the first two books. In this poetry book, "*The Healing*," I will take you on to a poetic journey, much more in depth, than what I had wrote about in *Mirrors and Reflections*. I have seen many things in the thirty years of my life on this earth. But never could I have imagined what was to come, especially in the year 2020. With this coronavirus disease, basically colonizing the entire planet, making its' way into America, we have never experienced something like this in our lifetime.

None of us really knew how to prepare for something like this; one minute someone is hugging their friends and family, the next minute, that person is coughing and sneezing excessively, and next thing you know, that person is fighting for their lives on a hospital bed. Some, however, did not make it off that hospital bed alive. What on earth was this all about?

Out there in the world, I am actually a man of very few words. Some would say I am quiet, and they would be precise, I am a quiet man. However, I do have a voice, and I do have something to say. Even though it may not be a voice in person, I can and will say what is on my mind in this book. I believe that social media has given so many people a platform, that it is rather difficult to have a voice of importance, a voice that people will consistently listen to, and feel that they are receiving some logical, relevant information. Social media has become a far cry from the truth. I am no longer on social media; I have no accounts, no presence, or no purpose to remain active. I felt that I no longer had a voice on Facebook, Instagram, Snapchat, or Twitter. I felt as if my voice was lost in the shuffle on those sites. No one truly is able to understand you through technology, in my opinion.

By me logging off of social media, I started the healing process. The healing process is still a work in progress, but I have achieved so much since I logged off two years ago. Even though I was never really a talker; I am most definitely a thinker, very observant, and I am able to express myself, confidently and unapologetically.

Now I must be honest with you, this particular book, "The Healing," this came out of nowhere. I was actually in the process of writing another book called, "*A Hidden Voice in America*." But you know what? I believe the universe did not want me to have that one just yet. It was not ready for me to deliver that kind of content. So, I listened to my intuition, I listened to the universe, and the universe blessed me with writing this book instead. I believe that this is not the right time to write a political book, this is a time to write a book of healing. I guess you could say that I needed some healing myself.

I am really proud of this book. This book is one that I believe is much needed in people's lives. This is a new collection of poetry, for you, the reader. Now, of course not all of the poems in this book are poems of healing. Some are for entertainment, long stories, short stories, and some dark twisted stories. But for the most part, I believe you will connect with quite a few of these poems. I really wanted to create more stories, to grow my body of work, and reach out to an expanding audience of readers.

One other thing; my anxiety has been at an all-time low, once I escaped the social media world. But after seeing what I am seeing, on video; all these African American people, being shot and killed, or having a knee pressed on top of an African American man's neck, for eight minutes and forty-six seconds, it makes me wonder if I am living in an actual country, or has America simply become a living hell, especially for African American people, along with other minorities.

I think what really terrifies me, is not specifically that my life is on the line, but the fact that many of our leaders do not have an answer. Leaders in their forties, fifties, sixties and seventies, they have no answers for their people. But our people are really fed up, overly sick and tired of the social injustices, systematic racism, oppression, and minorities lives not being worth a damn in this country. White supremacists rallying around the country, spreading such a tainted message, refusing to give up this polluted standard of "white supremacy."

If we as Americans continue to ignore our problems, if we continue to justify police brutality and racial profiling, America will not live to see it's 300th birthday. Have any of you realized that America is not even three centuries old yet? Compared to other countries worldwide, America is still a dream. It is still a work in progress. I wonder what the founding fathers of America would have to say about their country today. I seriously doubt they would be pleased. In fact, I believe they would be appalled at how regressive their country has become. I am sure that Washington, Hamilton, Franklin, Adams, Jefferson, Madison, Jay, Hancock, and even Abigail Adams would be entirely disappointed at how this country that they had a vision for, did not follow through for all the American people.

I will say this right now, the poetic journey that I have waiting for you after you read this introduction, I hope you do find some healing through this, some peace, and escapism.

As you read, I want you to understand that you are a human being, who's been through rough times in reality. Traumatic experiences that does not go away as easily as people may think. Mental health is such a must for all of us. I understand that we cannot just snap our fingers and turn all the wrong things right. We cannot compel ourselves to all get along and always treat each other nicely, no matter how many laws are passed in this country. As I said, we are human beings. We all have our flaws, we have our breaking points, and we definitely are not perfect.

But I will tell you what we do have, and that is potential. We all have the potential to make our country great, as well as the world, without prejudice, without hatred, and without racial profiling. But we cannot achieve greatness, if we do not have hope. I understand how dangerous of a word "hope" is, but as I said in my first book, "Logged Off," hope is a muscle we must train. We have to build hope in this country, we have to get hope stronger. How do we do that you may ask? We build hope through our actions, through changed behavior, and how we treat each other, regardless of what walks of life we are coming from.

In this book, "*The Healing,"* I did not divide them in sections. I have a prelude and an interlude. I just want you to enjoy yourselves, when you are reading this book. All I ask of you, the reader, regardless if you are Caucasian, African American, Asian, Latino, Middle eastern; you are still human. I ask you to give this a chance, give it a chance by just reading it. I believe it will be worthwhile, I do believe you will gain some healing from this poetry book. I welcome you into another journey, another trip inside my mind. But before we get to the healing, we must go through the pain.

Prelude

The Pain

I know I should not even have to ask this question; I think I already know the answer. But I will go ahead and ask anyway. Have you ever experienced pain? Yes, of course you have. We all have experienced pain. Whether that is physical pain, emotional pain, psychological pain, or we have given pain to someone else. It is in us; as much as we do not like pain, we secretly need it. We need pain to appreciate the pleasure. We need pain to understand that something is not quite right in our lives. We need pain to express our emotions, and our thoughts. We would not know what pleasure is without pain. Pain is built within all living creations.

I feel that most of the pain in today's world, it comes from the social dynamics that takes place online, through social media. Some of us have endured in cyberbullying, negative comments, racist videos, harassment, physical and domestic abuse. But pain is what makes us strong in this life.

It makes us appreciate what we have and who we have in our lives. We appreciate our friends, family, and even our pets. We go through pain, but pain is just a journey you must survive and not remain within it. So many people in this world are stuck in pain and misery, and people do get lonely within the pain and misery, which is why those people would love to have some company.

I remember when I fell in love for the first time. It was real, it was beautiful, but it was short lived. The heartbreak, the pain, that was definitely real. But I believe I may have stayed in that pain and misery longer than I should have. I stayed in that pain for three years. I knew that I had to let go and move forward in life, because my life was beginning to deteriorate. Self-love was non-existent to me at that time. But time, in this case, did heal the wound.

Do you understand me so far? Can you relate in any way? Pain and misery were like the right and left earphones, blasting in my ear, irregular frequencies, throwing my whole spirit off. Pain; there will be times in life that you will experience it. But that is okay, you will be okay. Because even though pain could come at random, uninvited and unsolicited; understand that it is not there to stay. Only you can choose to stay in pain and misery.

I mentioned social media before. Social media is what refueled the pain and misery that I suffered in, mentally, for many years. I felt if I just stayed on those platforms, stayed in that pain and misery, I basically would have defined myself as a victim, and victimization would have become my whole existence in life. Do not ever allow pain to define you in life. Pain is just a journey, destined to find its way into all of our lives at some point.

Let me ask you; which type of pain do you feel is the worst? The physical or the mental? That is a tough one, huh? Or maybe not, some may say that mental pain is the most painful. I would agree, mental pain can last for years, but then again, it depends on if people choose to stay in that pain and misery.

As I said on the back cover of this book, "*the pain will win some battles, but the love will always win the war*." Life is not just pain and misery. No matter what you see on the news or read in an article on the internet or social media. I would even say that in some cases, you can define what pain is to you. If you decide that seeing negative comments on your post are no longer going to contribute to your pain. You can decide that pain can sometimes be defeated, by mind over matter. But by no means am I trying to project that you should not have any empathy, compassion, or sympathy for others. You may have friends and family who are going through some things, and they may need your help.

But even then, you must be careful when people are in pain and are asking for help. Because help could potentially be an RSVP into their party of pain and misery. Remember, people alone in pain and misery, loves company. With all of that being said, let us get into these poems that I have prepared for you. I want to start you off with a couple of poems that I wrote, at the wee hours of the night. I woke up from a bad dream, I only remembered a few seconds from the dream, so I wrote what I could remember. But I am glad I woke up early that night. Because I ended up writing this particular poem in one shot.

It is a poem about fame. A fictional celebrity who endures in such pain; pain that only a star could understand. I feel that this poem will be a good start into, "*The Healing*." The name of the very first poem, "*She's Famous*."

"Oh, one thing I must mention before you begin. There is a poem in this book called, "Queen Virgin." You will read it later on. I thought it would be necessary to give a fair warning to you, the reader, that it contains some sexually explicit dialogue, with graphic imagery, that may not be suitable for anyone under the age of 17 or 18. Now of course, I know some of you are now going to skip over and read it now. But as long as I gave the warning now, I feel it should be okay."

She's Famous (08/06/20 4:44 a.m.)

She looks in the mirror, to a tear-stained face,
A night she'll hate to remember, she has to get out of this place.
She gathers her things, limo is waiting in front of the lobby,
She puts on a fake smile, it's now her new hobby.
Her fans are outside, cameras and phones are ready,
TMZ guy with the burning questions, keep the camera steady.
Shades to cover her anxious eyes,
Here comes the questions, she delivers the lies.
She takes some selfies with fans, then bodyguards create a wall,
She feels so trapped and imprisoned by this life, she can't escape at all.
Thousands of clicks, those selfies are already on the gram,
Negative comments as she scrolls, she thought they were her fans.
Her brain is filled with empty thoughts, only four hours of rest,
On her way to an interview, she has to look her best.
Out the limo, more fans and phones,
"No pictures right now, thank you," she now walks and talks with a frustrated tone.

Sitting in her dressing room, again she gazes at the mirror,
She's ready to breakdown and scream, but who, who will hear her?
She just wants to cry, and cry, and cry for the rest of her youth,
They just continue to lie, and lie, and lie for the rest of her truth.
What's going on in her bright, but naive brain,
While the social media world is calling her crazy, absolutely insane?
She tries to go live, and pleads her case,
My God, if you could just see the devastating look on her face.
Vertical comments saying, "JUST DIE YOU FAKE BITCH,"
She sees it, she ignores it, she can't scratch into the trolling, clout chasing itch.
She's about to be interviewed, but about last night?
I didn't mention her bruised eye from a physical fight.
A fight with who, you may be thinking?
A fight with her boyfriend, who was heavily drinking.
He pours his jealousy in a glass fragile ego,
She was pushing him off her, screaming, "let me go, let me go!"
A swing and a miss, another swing and it lands,

But this isn't the first time her face was invaded by a man's hand.
Daddy issues becomes mental issues,
Going into the interview saying, "can I have some tissue?"
In the interview they asked her, "what is it like to have fame?"
She responded truthfully saying, "it's a game, it's just a game."
She's rich, she's famous, but her happiness went so left, so wrong,
Yet she prays, tells her boyfriend to stay away, and gives her fans another hit song.

"You do not have time in life to make friends with people who already declared themselves your enemy."

A Bad Dream (08/06/20 3:23 a.m.)

I could feel that I was sleep,

I was half awake, the R.E.M was not as deep.

I saw these horrifying pictures of the letter Y,

I saw these monsters; I don't know why.

Sleep paralysis; ever had that?

Felt like a demon was creeping over my back.

I woke up completely, the dream lasted but a minute,

I stared at my ceiling fan, its shaped like a Y when I don't spin it.

This dream was so strange, where did it come from?

Dreams are strange period; there's so quick, only remember some.

It's like a match that was scratched, then the flame swiftly blew out,

Not enough information, burning questions, what was that all about?

"America's freedom of speech has become the freedom of ignorance. The second amendment has become people's first choice of how to handle altercations."

Strange Humans (7/13/20)

We don't have all the answers,

Why, oh why is there the curse of cancer?

Death is our in definite, don't bother to ask it,

Born to die like a pregnant casket.

Flesh and blood, two eyes and a brain,

Our tears can't compete with the rain,

Our tears water the flowers of our pain.

Broken bones, broken promises, broken rules,

Common sense drowning in our broken thoughts of an incompetent pool.

Fame is to blame for this bankrupt game,

Remember many faces, forget many names.

Marvin, I don't know what's going on,

Seeds of bullets planted in our bodies, a garden of death, but who's mowing the lawn?

Ego to your friends, amigo to your enemies,

Backs are turned, betrayal is earned, too late for remedies.

We hate funerals but they love us, who's next?

Is it a wheel of unfortune or already written in God's text?

I'm still breathing, we both have 24, we're even,

I just believed in me, believed in God, ask yourself who do you believe in?

Love is all we wish, yet it's so hard to find,

Even harder to keep, heartbreaks my mind.

You live in fear, once or twice a year,

You live courageous, because of your wealthy wages, lying tongues to gullible ears.

Stealing money from the weak-minded who confined,

Where's your heart, your soul? Like the tin man, nothing inside it.

Strange humans; where do we come from, what is our purpose?

At birth and on our death bed, we see doctors and nurses.

Nowhere to run, nowhere to hide,

Waking up in the morning, the internet showing us who died.

Smartphones have our souls, our time, our brains,

All it takes to go viral, is to go absolutely insane.

Social media go away; no stay, no just go,

Likes and hateful comments from random strangers you don't even know.

Scrolling their thumbs until they go numb,

Negative comments from negative people saying, "oh you're stupid dumb."

Free thinkers with empty minds; speak too fast to think twice,

Doesn't cost you a dime, feel free to be nice.

Nice to others; mothers and brothers,

Strange humans; we are like no other.

2020

(02/20/20 7:00 PM)

The horns are growing on this presidential tyrant,

Unsolicited crash in the fog; nine lives; my God, not Gianna and Kobe Bryant.

Covid-19; where'd you come from?

Cough once, sneeze twice, must have it, better run.

Kaepernick once took a knee, for a minute and a half song,

Racist cop took a knee on George Floyd's neck; 8 minutes and 46 seconds; America, you're dead fucking wrong.

Quarantine minded soldiers had enough, riots on the streets,

Watch your back brothers and sisters, those bullets love fresh meat.

Protesters screaming, police looking like Sparta's 300, with frowns and grins,

All we ask for is justice, make these cowards pay for their deadly sins,

America is losing, it's dying; hope is growing scarcely thin,

How much evil can a racist man or woman really hold deep within?

Black lives matter was the coupon for looters,

Secoriea Turner; 8-year-old baby girl, why you evil cowards have to shoot her?

Black lives won't matter if black lives pull the triggers,

America is getting sicker; cases grow frequently bigger.

Coronavirus is still out there, sneaking into the lungs of the human race,

Distractions on our brains, 6ix9ine was winning in first place.

Bullshit suicides; black men hanging from a tree,

Stop insulting my intelligence America, I know you're trying to kill me.

Now white politicians want to take a knee, after a knee killed a black man, this can't be,

Their kneeling legs reminds me of the Swastika, or is it just me?

Multi-cultural marching; the youth is the truth,

Tear gas, rubber bullets, police batons swinging away; the tainted reincarnation of Babe Ruth.

2020; Gemini year of Dr. Jekyll Mr. Hyde,

By the time you finish reading this, another unarmed African American man has just died.

A bi-polar year it has tragically been,

The devil was so busy; he couldn't lose, we couldn't win.

Election time has come; Trump and Covid-19 wants a second term in November,

Red pill, blue pill; no more orange peeled chicken, illegal tender,

Dear God, we the people just want to survive, all the way to the 31st of December.

Run as fast as you can to the 21st anniversary of Y2K,

Protect your mental health, protect your life, day by day.

THE HEALING

Fear is no longer an option, we have to survive,

The riddle is, "how do we stay black, as well as stay alive?"

The answer is God's wrath,

He's showing us the way, we're finding God's path.

The tears we saw,

The time has come to pass these laws,

The injustices are up and down like seesaws,

Never seen nothing like the year we saw,

Like uncle Charla says, "give this year the BIGGEST HEE HAW!"

"When it comes to social media, you're welcoming people to offend you. You're welcoming them to upset you and bully you. Every time you log on you're saying, "offend me!"

A Changed Man (07/14/20 11:18 PM)

Hell is in his mind, raising flames in his consciousness, but can't raise his kids,

Wallet on empty, nothing but his fingers in his pocket, nowhere to dig.

A father of two, but works three jobs,

One a burger is flipping; two the phone is ringing, and three, looking for someone to rob.

The streets say they love him, yet the streets lie,

The streets are a concrete vampire, they want his blood soaking in the pavement, they want him to die.

He doesn't see his kids, he doesn't see the future,

Mother of his kids, their ups and downs she forgives, he almost tried to shoot her.

One day he flips the burger, compared the burger to his life,

Imagining if he flipped his life around, he could change, baby momma would make a great wife.

High school diploma is out of the question; G.E.D is the answer,

His mother's lifelong wish was for him to graduate, before she died of cancer.

Out on the streets since he was 16, father wasn't there,

The streets were his school, survival was education, got arrested before he grew facial hair.

An idea splashed in his head, put out the fire to those flames,

No more robbing, no more streets, no more hustling and dice games.

A changed man, forgive him lord for his darkest sins,

A changed man, striving to manifest his greatest potential within,

A changed man, who's ready to achieve, ready to win.

He's changed; a better father to his kids, a better man,

Every morning he wakes up, he sees his Obama poster saying, "yes we can!"

Looking in the mirror, fixing that tie, he walks out the door,

His three jobs, have now grown to a new four,

Fatherhood, Ambassador, Motivator, Entrepreneur.

He's famous now, catch him if you can,

But he's not running from the cops anymore, he is a changed man.

Therapy Session (07/13/20 4:46 AM)

The more ideas I am granted, the more insane I become,

Forgive me for my insanity, the birth of a God has begun.

Orbit me forever, I am your sun,

Swimming in this dark universe, gravitational pull of billions of tons.

Tell me you love me, I demand it, I need it,

I'm scared to be alone; I'll feel so defeated.

I close my eyes, hope to dream,

Chaotic collage, why are nightmares so mean?

Fear is trying to rob me of a good life I can enjoy,

Fear is trying to sabotage my manhood, pull me back to that scared little boy.

I can't sleep, no use in counting sheep,

I'm a wolf howling; is the moon too far, or too deep?

I drown in my thoughts, and I love it,

I die with genius in my brain, my veins, remember my name, oh I love it!

Can't stop listening to Ye's music, it's making me brilliant,

Life broke his jaw, his heart; he broke records and broke through, Ye is too resilient.

Life is a canvas, painted with your actions,

Show the world your talent, peers give reactions.

I am a gifted genius, I share with you my knowledge and wisdom,

Crack open my books; step into my lair, my kingdom.

But I can't be a genius without you, forgive me if I didn't wrap it,

I wish anxiety had a face, so I can always slap it.

Not perfect, flaws are my distant relatives,

I killed my regrets; no need for an investigation or detectives.

I can't help this, perhaps it's a gift, and that's okay,

Thank you for your time, for listening to what I have to say.

We're Still Friends (07/13/20 4:37 AM)

It's true, Heart break is what you caused me,

All these years of ups and downs, the flaws of you and me.

I wanted more than a kiss on the cheek,

I opened my heart to you, you saw me when I was strong, but ignored me when I've been weak.

I felt alone in my life; alone, alone, alone,

Like a mirror with no one to reflect, a mirror without a home.

Picked me up when you got bored, put me down when you were too busy,

Another guy in the picture, but where's Waldo? Who is he?

Instagram is the instinct instigator,

You would have broken my heart, sooner or later.

Sex was in last place while love was in first,

I fed off the hugs and kisses; I overdosed; I was about to burst.

Our arguments created currents instead of ripples,

We were close like breast, but not as free like nipples.

A phone with seizures kept your focus away from me,

Frustrated with your lack of attention; I'm not a ghost, can't you see?

It will never be the same, a completely different game,

I hate the fact that every time you moan, you're not saying my name.

Don't call me jealous, I'm not even curious,

I was never mad; hearts are too fast and furious.

Our chance died prematurely, but our bond survives,

I'll be happy to see the birth of your motherhood, when your first born arrives.

We're still friends, after all these years, how could that be?

You satisfy my soul, knowing that you'll always love me.

Forgive and Dismiss (07/21/20 2:12 PM)

The shock; her heart was racing at a frightening pace,

The aftershock of her man's hand slashed across her face.

The look on his face, the look in his eyes,

All she wanted was for him to tell the truth, not the consistent lies.

Her heart once filled with love, now filled with fear,

The beast has been released, she can't hold her anxious tears,

She looks down; her hand has become a stained canvas of her blood; oh dear.

Ten years with her lover, who's now this stranger,

His abusive true colors are exposed, her life is now in danger.

Love with a fist; a toxic formula that confuses her,

How can she see love when this love is what abuses her?

Scary thoughts in her mind; should she stay, or should she leave?

He begs for her to stay, crying he'll never hit her again; that she can't believe.

She grabs her bags and runs as he screams, his devilish yells,

She doesn't need this life; this is her living in hell.

Rising flesh on her bruised cheekbone,

Calling the police; she has them on speakerphone.

"My man just attacked me, I don't know what to do,"

"Okay ma'am, cops are on the way, is he still there with you?"

"No, I'm driving, two blocks away from my home,"

"Okay ma'am, just stay put, give us your location, and don't hang up the phone."

Her phone shivers from multiple text,

It is him, her brand-new abusive ex.

She's never seen so many apologies all at once, begs her not to go,

"Please baby, please! I'm sorry, I need you;" but her answer is no.

"Baby please, I love you. The other girl, she's just a friend,"

This is the text she made before she pressed send.

"*Never in my darkest times, my deepest fears, my saddest days,*

Did I ever think you would put your hands on me and treat me in the worst way.

You were my heart, my soul, my best friend,

It breaks my heart that this will be the very end.

You've lost my trust, you've lost my love,

As far as forgiveness; you must beg the man from above.

I can never take you back, I don't even want to try,

So, this is where I take my leave from you, this where I say goodbye."

He Survived A Night of Blue Suits (6/28/20)

That siren; flickering of red and blue,

That's all he saw, looking at the mirror of his rear view.

A blue suit figure makes way to the driver's door,

"Licenses and registration," not a tone of please, but a tone of order.

Blue suit heads back to his car, ten minutes goes by,

Driver grows worried; too many videos of police killing unarmed black guys.

Five minutes more, driver now recording on his phone,

Blue suit comes back to the driver's door, now with a more intense law and order tone.

"Step outside the car," still there's no please,

"Hands behind your head now, get on your knees."

"What did I do officer? I've committed no crime,"

"Keep your mouth shut, don't resist, and you'll be fine."

Back up arrived, one blue suit became five,

The driver, he looks around, afraid he won't make it out of this alive.

Aggressive takedown; his hands cuffed behind his back,

A thousand thoughts going on in his mind, of being the next victim of a deadly police attack.

"I have my wife and kids, I haven't done anything,"

Five blues suits surrounded him, formed a circle, a ring,

Driver is having a déjà vu, another Rodney King.

"Dear God, if you're watching, please protect my family and friends,

I have a bad feeling that this will be the very end."

He fears they're going to choke him, arms and knees are the new noose,

One blue suit stands him up, uncuffed him, lets him loose.

Original blue suit gives him his papers and said, "you're free to go,"

Driver's heart is racing, goosebumps on his dark skin crawling slow,

Blinded justice; the red and blue lights makes his face glow.

He goes back into his car, eyes drenched of falling tears,

His whole life flashed before his eyes, quick flash of just 27 years.

The Crown Vic wagons take off, leaving him in the dark,

He needed a minute to calmly collect himself, he leaves his car in parked.

He screams to the top of his lungs,

Understands why Kaepernick kneeled every time the Star-Spangled Banner was sung.

He's looking for his phone, left it on his dashboard mount,

He realized he left his camera on, recorded it all, every amount.

The verbal and physical abuse is in the eye of the iPhone beholder,

He drives home, can't wait to be with his kids and wife, can't wait to hold her.

His babies were sleep, his wife was awake with desperate concern,

He said, "baby, my night could have taken such a fatal turn."

He tells the brutal story, four eyes crying thousands of tears, they are each other's tissues,

She said, "we have to do something about these social injustices, we have to fix these issues."

He wiped her tears and said, "I recorded it, it's all on my phone,

I just thank God I survived it; I thank God I made it home."

"The camera does not lie, but people do, and they will lie on camera."

Matches and Flames (08/06/20 3:52 a.m.)

Matches of ideas, but too afraid to scratch its head,

Too afraid to give birth to burning questions, the match stays red.

One Spark of flame, you must grow it,

Only one light to live, don't blow it.

A swimming of flames, but there is no water flow,

Miles away, you can still see flames glow.

Smoke; the Cologne of death,

You inhale it too much, let that be your last breath.

One horizontal kiss, flame in love, make it count,

A flick of a lighter, unfaithful to the match, flames of an unlimited amount.

For every birthday there is a flame blown out,

Be careful what you wish for, it just might turn out.

"When I see what the nation is doing with these statutes and flags, it reminds me of the same thing the dream team did with O.J. Simpson's house, when they removed all the photos of Simpson with white people and replaced them with African artifacts. They are just hiding the harsh reality of American history. But the white supremacy will still be in the minds of many. Do I disagree with the removal of some of these statutes, no. However, if people believe that will change America, they would be inaccurate."

I Remember You (08/1/20 10:31 PM)

I turned the corner, there you were,

Oh my God, I can't believe it is her.

Curly long hair, a complexion like mines,

Maybe she's the one, it is only a matter of time.

A brief talk we had, a brief kiss we made,

Memories short lived, the moments began to fade.

Our arguments made me sick, hard to recover,

I'm alone now, while you have found another lover.

Even if I could turn back the clock, I still couldn't make it right,

I close my eyes and see you, it's like love at first sight,

We text from the morning, to the end of the night.

Heartbreaks are the worst cakes to bake,

The recipe of rejection was too salty, how much more could I take?

It all started with a post I made about Drake.

Perhaps if I was; no, it just wasn't meant to be,

I was too blinded by ambition, to really think you'd be with me.

I said my goodbyes, I just want you to be happy,

I had to escape before the regrets entrapped me.

Who cares, right? All of what you been through,

For what it's worth, I may never see you again, but I'll still remember you.

Let's Get This Straight (07/31/20 8:49 PM)

I'm not your nigga, that's a death wish,
Remove that from your lake of vocabulary, that's a bad fish.
I'm walking down the street, you walk to the other side,
As if I am an instant threat, how do you think that makes me feel on the inside?
I am not your enemy, I am a human being,
What is going on in your mind, what is it that you're not seeing?
I walk in a store, following me around, thinking I'm going to steal,
Once again, how do you think that makes me feel?
I am not a criminal, a thief, or a crook,
Stop following me around the store, don't give me that look.
I am highly educated, your ignorance is not welcomed,
By any means necessary, I will continue to strive, like Malcolm.
You think I'm a thug, walk pass me and you're filled with fear?
Remind me; who were the group of people who enslaved and murdered others for 400 years? 500 years?
Oh, now you have absolutely nothing to say?
No apologies? No reparations to pay?
Okay.

"The psychology of racism is a statute of thought, that must be brought down. The consciousness of people's prejudices must be destroyed. Never mind the statues of historical figures."

Cuddles and Ice Cream (07/31/20 2:23 AM)

The couch so comfy, like a soft and billowing cloud,
Bring it down a few knots, the television's too loud.
I lay on the couch first, she pressed her back to my chest,
I gently wrapped my arms around her, in desperate need of rest.
My face disappeared in her majestic garden of hair,
It felt like a dream, she was my gypsy, and I was her dancing bear.
A brief disconnection, she comes back with ice cream,
Back in my arms, her hands are cold, if you touch me there, I'll scream.
I melt faster than that ice cream, the way she plays with her spoon,
Take me away, to a starry night, let's both kiss the moon.
A spoonful scoop flying in mid-air, landing on my tongue,
A frost bite taste, plus a French kiss, she left me sprung.
Ice cream lipstick made its way all over my face,
Her cookies and cream breath gave me chills, as if I was in outer space.
How did I get so lucky; two desserts at the same time,
We murdered that ice cream; like Bonnie and Clyde, she's my partner in crime.

"Our anger is a bullet; our ignorance is a knife."

#Mental Health (07/20/20 12:27 AM)

The traffic of trauma, the traffic pain,
Thoughts crashing all over, self-destruction in the brain.
Can't sleep, reality is too real,
Numb to death, can't talk, can't feel.
No calling people crazy, social media has the world running oh so lazy,
Can't see straight, poisoned perceptions, the world is oh so hazy.
Bi-polar is winning, in a league of its own,
People walking around aimlessly, people walking in the twilight zone.
Depression at every scroll, get off the gram,
Save your brain cells from mental enslavement, I repeat, get off the gram.
The mind is a terrible thing to confuse,
What's the point of gaining the world, but your mind you lose?
Manipulation moving slow, but succeeding fast,
Nightmares and anxiety double teaming your mind with your past.
Hiding our pain right in plain sight,
Hallucinations bullying our brains in the night.
People call people crazy, but what is to blame?

Childhood, deaths, the whole social media game?
9 to 5 jobs for decades, non-livable pay,
No one to talk to, at the end of the day.
I'm not giving up on my brother, not giving up on Ye,
Hug him, talk to him, whatever it takes, let us pray.
Help is available, help is out there,
There are people who love you, there are people who care.
Please learn to love yourself, even if it takes a while,
Life is a struggle, but still worth living like a Stephen
Hawking smile.

Possession and Desire (07/17/20 10:27 PM)

I fiend for your undying fragrance,

I longed for your loneliness,

My jealousy is my addiction, my curse.

You punish my temptation of another woman's flesh,

Kiss me to death so that I can reincarnate into eternal bliss, with you.

I am possessed by you, I beg you not to release me,

Imprison me in your possession, no need for bars, I shall never escape.

Look at me; please look at me.

Manifest my fantasies of you,

My desires would kill to be fulfilled.

"No" is the wall that divides us, please say yes.

Say yes to destroy my temptation,

Or say no to kill me; over, and over, and over, and over again.

I promise if you promise, a promise for today.

Never trust a promise for tomorrow when tomorrow is not promised.

But if I was tomorrow, I'd promise you would see me.

If I could; I would change my name to tomorrow.

That way I would always promise, that you'll have me, and always see me.

"Do you know who really runs the world? The FDA; not the FDA you may be thinking of, but this FDA.

Fashion, Doctors, and Attorneys."

The Most Twisted Story

You Will Ever Read (07/25/20 6:28 PM)

She's married, the love of her life waits,
A short walk away from dinner, any longer she'll be late.
A hazy figure stands far from her, 30 feet apart,
Closer and clearer he becomes, my God, it is her high school sweetheart.
She can't believe her eyes, haven't seen him in years,
He can't get over how beautiful she is, the chilly air of dusk creates mixed feeling tears.
Two adults, four hands, only one with a ring,
He sees she's taken, new heartbreak, same old sting.
He lost her all over again, a forbidden Deja vu,
Yet she's stuck in her heart, she doesn't know what to do.
A buzzing from the bottom of her hoarding purse,
A husband's text, "sorry babe, have to cancel our date, mom's cough got worse.
A wife's reply, "oh no worries, I'll see you later tonight; kiss emoji,"
Looking at him with unfaithful thoughts, "God, I'd give anything for him to kiss and hold me."
A cancelled date, she's no longer late,

Her first love staring right at her; dear God, is this fate?

He takes her by the hand, they go for a lingering walk,

Talking, laughing; reminiscing about writing "I Luv U" on the board with pink chalk.

Time flies, she doesn't want it to land,

Time to call it a night, but she doesn't let go of his hand.

He looks at her and says, "I'm sorry, but I do have to go,"

She looks up at him with the saddest of puppy eyes and says, "NO."

"What about your husband? It's a sin to cheat,"

She responded, "I know, I know; but it has to be a sign, why else did we unexpectedly meet?"

"You're a married woman, you and I was in the past,"

She said, "I didn't want it to end, I loved you, but you always put me last."

The guilt gives his voice a struggling tone,

"I'm so sorry, I was in a dark place, I just wanted to be alone."

She wiped her eyes and said, "forgiveness is bliss,"

He brought her face to his, for an unforgettable midnight kiss.

Heartbreak recovers, her husband's nowhere in sight,

Hotel room, here they come; it's going to be an adulterous night.

Opened morning eyes, she doesn't see her husband's face,

THE HEALING

Eyes filled with tears of instant regret; she has to get out of this place.
She doesn't want to wake him, leaves him a goodbye note with her number, I wonder why?
Got dressed quickly and quietly, out the door, in the elevator; an uncontrollable cry,
The tears can't turn back the clock, preparing to give her husband the ultimate lie.
Home at last, ran straight to the shower,
Trying to wash off her pleasures of sin, stayed in for at least an hour.
The running shower couldn't keep up with her tears,
Crying so loudly, shhh! Her husband hears.
Hubby knocks on the door, "baby, you're okay?"
She said, "Yes baby, I'm good; I'll be right out, okay?"
He says, "I'm sorry I didn't make it home, spent the night at my mother's,"
She began to cry some more; guilty she spent the night with a significant other.
She looks in the misty mirror, can't see or feel a thing,
Somethings missing on her hand; oh my God, it's her diamond ring.
She hurries to empty out her hoarding bag,
No ring, no idea, no voice, she's about to gag.
Her phone rings; ten feet from her, two inches from her man,

She is shaking as if she saw a ghost; he answers it, and he turned to look at her hand.
She knows it's her first love, big mistake in leaving her number and a goodbye note,
Her husband says, "oh thanks dude, I'll let her know, that's dope."
He hangs up and she cautiously ask, "who was that, let me see?"
He said, "oh that was the guy at the jewelry store, he's cleaning your wedding ring for free?"
She says with confusion and relief, "oh, I didn't know it's free, that's dope,"
He responded, "Yea, that's what I just said. Oh, but he left this note."
She asked, "what did the note say,"
The note said, "if there's ever a time when you need to turn back the clock, it's only but a number away."
Her first love reiterated the goodbye note she left at the hotel,
Her secret is safe with him, she knows he will never tell.
She cracks a smile while cracking some eggs for breakfast,
She can't believe her night, right out of a movie on Netflix.
She thinks in her mind if they will ever reunite in this life of sin?
A dangerous game she is playing; another message, it's him.

He says, "that was a close one, next time I'll be careful when
I call or text,"
She replied, "I appreciate it, but now I think it's best that
there be no next."
He responded in all caps, "WHAT DO YOU MEAN?!"
She said, "last night was beautiful, but when I woke up, it just
felt like a bad dream."
He says, "don't do this to me again, don't break my heart,"
Tears dropping on her smartphone screen, she text, "I can't
leave my husband, it would tear him apart."
He responded, "I don't want to say goodbye, we saw each
other again for a reason,"
She said, "I made a bad choice, I cheated on my husband,
I've committed treason."
Her heart got as cold as her untouched eggs,
30 texts later, his obsession grows, he uncontrollably begs.
She steps out with her phone, calls and says, "look, forget this
happened, I just want my ring!"
He says, "you're a liar, a cheat, you don't deserve that ring!"
She screams, "don't piss me off, don't make this matter
worse,"
He says with uncontrollable laughter, "maybe you should
check the side of your purse."
He put it in the side compartment of her bag while she slept,
her ring is what she finds,

All this time she thought she lost it, but really, she was losing her mind.
Laughter swimming in her ear, she tells him to never call her in this life,
He called her a bitch more times than she can count, calling her a sorry excuse for a wife.
Back in her house she goes, she sees her husband crying on the bed,
She says, “baby what’s wrong? Oh my God, your mother; is she dead?”
He says, “no, but there is something I think you must know,”
She says, “I have something to tell you too, but you first, you go!”
Tears wiped as he says, I don’t know where to start or how it will end,”
She tells him, “just tell me the truth, don’t lie, don’t pretend.”
He says, “last night, I wasn’t at my mother’s, I made other plans,”
She’s confused, “wait, what? Baby, I don’t understand.
What do you mean you had other plans?”
Tears gently declining down his face,
Both hearts are racing, but who’s going to win first place?
“Baby, tell me the truth, what was that other plan?”
He says, “I guess there’s no other way to put it; I was out, with another man.”

She gags yet again, “what the fuck are you trying to say?”
He tells her with ease, “I’m so sorry, but I am gay.”
She gives him a slap heard round the world; a nasty cut, he may need a stitch,
The moral of this twisted story is, Karma is indeed a bitch.

"Life is a moment of magic, a moment of mystery, and sometimes tragedy. I think what makes us strange is when things are going well for us, we find tragedy in it, and when tragic things happen, we find the humor, the joy, the happiness within the tragedy."

A Prayer (07/30/20 12:51 AM)

Two hands kiss, two eyes closed, let us pray,
Dear God; thank you for another day.
You gave us life, on your spherical land,
We come together to praise you, hand and hand.
We thank you, for you are the light to salvation,
The gate keeper to an eternal heavenly vacation.
You are forgiving of our sins,
You are the spirit within.
We thank you for your borrowed time of humankind,
We thank you for the blessings, for staying close, never hard to find.
We ask for your guidance if we are ever lost,
We thank you for leading us to serenity, no matter the cost.
We ask you that you continue to watch over us in the time of crucial need,
We ask that you protect us from temptation, deliver us from evil and greed.
We thank you for good health,
Negative energy in the air like stealth.
We ask that you give our leaders of the world direction,
We pray that you give us the strength during this 2020 election.
In God's name amen; open your eyes, disconnect your hands,

The more you connect with God, the better you will understand.

I Don't Have Her (08/15/20 2:25 PM)

We sat next to each other, Your shoulder next to mines,
Seems like it was so long ago, fun times.
You drink but I don't, twisted faces,
Short-lived moments in different places.
I like your hair, I envy your shampoo,
I drown in your perfume scented pool.
Your pool of presence, can I forever have your lips?
You make me melt to liquid, feel free to take a sip.
Give me all the drinks of hello, hold the ice of goodbye,
I'll get drunk off your greetings, don't leave me sober with melted cries.
You are just a memory now, a dream that didn't come true,
My dreams were misleading, reality kept proceeding, I wish I could sue.
We could have fallen in a deep ocean of love,
Grow wrinkled, the sparkling waters from above.
The truth I learned, we can't fall in love through a phone,
Unnatural arguments created an inhuman tone.
A breakup before the relationship began,
Now I don't have you, and I may never see you again.
My memories of you are like a rose in a bottle,
Every time I think of you, my heart goes into full throttle.

Do me a favor, if you ever care to try,

Read this poem, kiss the page, and cry your goodbyes.

He Wished Her A Sad Birthday (08/2/20 12:39 AM)

She looks at the diner clock, the big hand surpassed 10 o'clock,
Her birthday is wasting away, tick tock, tick tock,
He's not responding to her calls, her stomach in knots,
She's text him saying, "the food has been served, hurry up and get while it's hot."
Still, she gets no answer, he's running late,
Not sure what's happening, he's never tardy for a date.
Finally, he texts her saying, "sorry babe, on my way, I'm not too far."
She responded, "okay babe, it's actually getting late, I'll pack our food, and just wait at the bar."
Another hour goes by, at the bar she waits,
Frustrated with him completely, she texts him saying, "wow, way to ruin my birthday, that's great!
She decided to leave, got in her car and slammed the door,
Tears dying down her cheek, she throws her phone on the floor.
Her watery eyes see the blinking light on her phone,
It is her mother, talking in a traumatizing tone.
She asked her mother, "Oh my God mom, what's wrong?"
Mom said, "Baby, he's in the hospital, I'll meet you there, I won't be long."

Instant shock to her body, her mind became a blank empty space,
More tears started dying, declining down on her face.
She drove as fast as she safely could, you'd think she's in a race,
Racing against time, no finish line, no first place.
She runs through the automatic doors, screaming, "where is he? Is he okay?"
Her mother then comes in behind her, hugs her and asks, "what did they say?"
She said emotionally, "I don't know, help me find him,"
The nurse looked up his name and said, "room 1111 is where they assigned him."
They both rushed to the elevator, pushing all the buttons,
But the elevator just stood there, didn't move, it did nothin.
They both ran up the stairs, it was two flights,
They made their way to the room, to see him there, my God, what a horrible sight.
A ring around the Rosie with his car, almost cost him his life,
She stands there in shock, in fear, that she won't get the chance to be his wife.
Doctors assured her that it's not as bad as it looks,
Her mother takes her out the room and says, "come here baby, don't look."
They waited, his family finally came through,

Lots of hugs, kisses and a thank you.
A horizontal line on the waiting room clock, a late night indeed,
The doctor finally comes to them and said, “my God, he really did bleed.”
His parents asked, “but he’ll live right?”
The doctor said, “oh of course, they’ll both be alright.”
Birthday girl thinks and says, “what do you mean both of them?”
Doctor explains, “there was a passenger in his car, a woman, it wasn’t just him.”
Are you thinking what she’s thinking? Mixed feelings began to grow in her mind,
Broken bones and broken promises, unbroken secrets are what she cracks open to find.
She asked the doctor if she could see this woman, her face,
The Doctor said, “sorry, but family only, and she needs her rest and space.
Things got stranger, this you can’t pretend,
Two familiar parents have arrived, the parents of her best friend.
She runs to them and ask, “what are you doing here?”
They tell her that her best friend was in a car accident, and asked her, what are you doing here?”
She followed the parents to her best friend’s hospital door,

She's putting two and two together, betrayal thoughts begin to soar.
Both parents hug their dazed daughter, but she recognized her best friend,
If you could see the look on the birthday girl's face, you'd know that friendship came to an end.
You see, the birthday girl text her best friend earlier asking, "come out, let's have some fun,"
She responded saying, "no, I have so many errands, by the time I get home, I'll be too tired and done."
The picture has been perfectly painted,
The poor birthday girl damn near fainted.
Her best friend was not out running errands as she said,
Her best friend was sleeping with her boyfriend, in his bed.
He was dropping her off, then heading to see the birthday girl,
Karma is such a bitch, took those two on car flipping twirl.
The birthday girl cries to her mother, "momma, please say this isn't true?"
Her mother says, "don't worry baby, this is something you'll get through."
Both of them exit the hospital, the sun is starting to rise,
Sad birthday, nothing happy, her face covered with dead makeup and cries.

A birthday she'll never forget, hope this one doesn't ruin the rest,
She'll be okay, she's resilient, she is the best.

"If you're chasing a dream or chasing a person who has too many demons attached to them, it is not worth it. But you know that already, right?"

Ali (08/4/2020 10:21 PM)

One square, four corners, the mic drops,
Ladies and gentlemen, the main event, cameras flickering and pops.
Two gloves in the air, shuffling feet,
He steps to his opponent, they finally meet.
The look in his eyes, pure concentration, back peddles to his ring side,
Standing and praying to Allah, his trainer whispered in his ear, "protect the inside."
The bell rings, it's showtime, here he comes,
Jab, jab; opponent doesn't see it coming, his face is a human drum.
His opponent is working on his body, Ali grabs him up,
"IS THAT ALL YOU GOT SUCKA?!" Ali says, trying to gas him up.
A haymaker to Ali's face, swing and a miss,
My how Ali dodged those punches, his elusiveness is of divine bliss.
The opponent hammers away at Ali's ribs, finally, there's the bell,
Opponent is gasping for air; Ali is putting him through hell.
Sitting in his corner, Ali winks and he stares,

His opponent realized that Ali is the lion, and the ring is his lair.
The bell rings, get ready for another round,
He's punching Ali like there's no tomorrow, hoping he hits the ground,
But Ali is taking them one by one, he's the greatest, pound for pound.
His opponent can't throw anymore, he has nothing left,
BOOM with the right, BOOM with the left,
Ali hit him with a combo, opponent hits the ground, all he sees are lights and the ref.
One, two, three, four, five,
The opponent can't move, he doesn't know if he's dead or alive.
Looking for his mouthpiece, it's on the other side of the ring,
The ref swinging his arms, "You're Out!" There's the bell; ding, ding, ding!
The crowd goes wild; blood, sweat, and tears on the ground,
Smoke in the air, look at Don King's hair, the real king is about to be crowned.
Hazy vision, the opponent can hear, but it's hard to see,
All he hears is, "STILL HEAVYWEIGHT CHAMPION OF THE WORLD, MUHAMMAD ALI!"

He Put Down the Drink (08/7/20 5:18 PM)

A glass bottle clinging onto the glass cup,
He tilts the filled glass down his mouth while his head lifts up.
It flows through his bloodstream, makes him feel good,
He has another, and another, but the third one, don't think he should.
He does; he's tilting, can't seem to walk straight,
He looks at his phone, a hazy vision, it's after midnight, it's late.
He can't think right now, can't pull himself together,
He hoped in his car, blowing the horn; like Lena, he's driving in stormy weather.
He's driving while intoxicated, a deadly weapon in a car,
A swerve here and there, he's stops, he doesn't go too far.
A million raindrops tapping on his car,
This relaxing sound puts him to sleep, sweet dreams thanks to ASMR.
Break of dawn, he opens his eyes, a headache for two,
The party's over; doesn't know where he is, he doesn't have a clue.
A loud notification from his phone, to him it sounds like an explosion,

He shuts off the noise, a message from his wife, the love and care she shows him,
He begins to cry, thanking God that she actually chose him.
She said, "baby, I'm so worried, I woke up and you didn't come home,"
He responded, "I'm so sorry hunny, I'm on my way, soon, you will not be alone.
By night, he was drunk by liquor, by day, he is drunk by guilt,
He's destroying his relationships, his marriage, and all the friendships he's built.
He finally made it home, his wife hugs him with the tightest grip,
A combination of tears and kisses from her worried eyes and concerned lips.
She cried, "please don't ever do this to me again, I thought you were dead, this time,
A thousand drunken thoughts intoxicated in his head; he looks over to his collection of wine.
He picks a bottle up, gives it a long lingering stare,
His mind tells him to pour a glass, but his spirit tells him, "don't you dare."
She looks at him, he looks at her; he has to make a choice,
He's tired of the drinking, he hates hearing his wife's heartbroken voice.

THE HEALING

He heals her broken heart by breaking the glass bottle against the wall,
He gets on one knee, tells his wife, “I’ll never pick up a drink again; no wine, no liquor, nothing at all.”
He pours his heart into her glass of forgiveness,
Promising her he won’t fake this; he will definitely live this.
She looks at him and said this without a blink,
“This is your last chance; I’m glad you decided to put down the drink.”

"People would ask you, "are you happy?" But the thing is, that is the wrong question to ask people. The real question; well, I should say the real statement that should be said is, "you are alive." You woke up this morning, you have another day at life, to make things right, sometimes with people who have done you wrong or who you've done wrong to. I believe happiness and sadness are moments of events in our lives, they are a presence, an experience. But they can never really define us."

Protect Your Innocence (08/6/20 12:27 AM)

Detective: Don't worry, you're in a safe place to talk,

Man: ....

Det: So, we know you were out at this time, where did you walk?

Man: ...

Det: I think it is beneficial for you to cooperate, don't tell no lies,

Man: ....

Det: We know you weren't alone; we have footage of you with three other guys.

Man: ....

Det: So, you're just going to sit there and not say a word?

Man: I want a lawyer,

Det: I guarantee you; you cooperate with us; you'll be free as a bird.

Man: I want a lawyer,

Det: We already have fingerprints, you might as well confess,

Man: I want a lawyer,

Det: You can play this game if you want to, but you'll be the one stress.

Man: I want a lawyer,

Det: Hey listen, I'm getting overtime, we can do this all night,

Man: I want a lawyer,

Det: Okay, you want to remain silent, I won't force you to talk. After all, you have the right.

Man: ....

The Oath (08/8/20 5:32 PM)

Nice mask; come in, have a seat,
Apologies for the delay, it's great that we finally meet.
I assume you understand why we hoodwinked you here,
But you mustn't be worried, show no fear.
We have a deal for you, an offer only a fool would refuse,
We have the power; but only you can choose.
We have it all; the fortune and the fame,
We can give that to you, as long as you play by the rules to the game.
Whatever you want; you ask, you shall receive,
We can give you a life you can only dream, fantasies you would not believe.
What do we want in return you may ask?
Here's the paper to your ultimate task.
We need your name signed in blood, all it takes is a small cut to slightly bleed,
We do not believe in fairness; we believe in ourselves; we believe in greed.
We are a family of loyalty, secrets are a must,
If you disclose our secrets, you burn our trust.
Prepare to lose if you break the rules,
Consequences are at hand; this world will become oh so cruel.

We have your number; it is already reserved,
You get out of line; you'll get what you deserve.
We own the media, we have eyes like the owl,
No questions of who, what, when, where, why, or how.
Watch what you post, what you tweet;
You give too much knowledge, once again we shall meet.
Once you sign; we own your voice,
We own your mind, your body, your soul, and you don't have a choice.
You have a talented gift, but only we make the stars,
We have the money, the power, riches and fabulous cars,
Come, join us; take The Oath, and we will take you far.
Please choose wisely, once you cross over, there is no going back,
You will never see the world the same again, that is a fact.
Thank you for attending our mansion party, we now ask that you take your leave,
But before you go, look into my eyes, and tell me what you see.

He Went After Her (08/8/20 8:20 PM)

Two voices, one unforgettable argument, she leaves,
A broken window; she threw her curling iron at him, it landed in the leaves.
He says, "don't ever come back," she says, "don't worry, I won't,"
In his mind he quickly thinks, "good," but in his heart he's says, "don't!"
She grabs her bags and keys and slams the door,
He yells out the window, "don't come back here no more!"
Tires burning the pavement, she hits the road,
Someone is calling, but his phone is on silent mode.
It was his friend, he gives his friend a call,
He screams, "I kicked her ass out, you two have fun, have a ball,"
His friend said, "you're so mistaken, your girl and I have nothing going on at all."
He responded, "I saw you text her, telling her to keep it a secret, secrets make me mad!"
His friend said, "well, I guess I have no choice but to tell you, you are going to be a dad!"
Stunned! Surprised at such life changing news,
Now he understands why she felt so nauseous, every time she chews.

He asked his friend, “why would she keep such good news from me?”
He said,” she wanted to keep it a surprise, for your anniversary.”
His guilt and jealousy got the best of him,
Now he’s afraid that she may think less of him.
His friend tells him, “find your woman, now you know,”
He hangs up and calls her; no answer, she left an hour ago,
He got dressed, grabbed his wallet and keys, out the door he goes.
He calls again, “I’m so sorry,” is the voice message he leaves,
He texts her saying, “I know now, I’m sorry, please come back to me.”
He gets an idea of where she could be,
He makes a U-turn and drives to the park where they will celebrate their anniversary.
He knows her too well, because she was there,
He could tell it was her, after the curling iron incident, she just did her hair.
He slowly walks behind her, he said, “baby, please forgive me.”
She turns around with her teary hazel eyes and said, “why did you have to ruin our anniversary?”
He fell to one knee, held her by her hips, and kissed her belly,

His glossy eyes of tears look at her and he said, “I know now, you don’t even have to tell me.”
She looks down at him and gave him the most beautiful, heartwarming smile,
An unforgettable anniversary night, a starry sky that stretched for miles.
Parents to be, thank God this wasn’t a massacre,
Remember this night, as the night that he went after her.

"*We are living in a time where people's ignorance has outnumbered them, which will eventually destroy them.*"

Mirror in The Morning (08/8/20 11:30 PM)

The dawn is breaking, her body is awakened,
Blessed to see another sunrise,
another beautiful painting of reality.
A steel blue-look inside an all-white painted room,
Wrapped in her covers as her hair is wrapped in a scarf,
Looking up at the ceiling, her fan twirling around like a propeller in an ocean of air.
Her eyes focused on a picture of her dad,
A disconnect; a relationship that crashed, sinking in thick betrayal.
She relocates the picture, stuffed in a closet of shame.
Her bare feet walking on a cold air-conditioned floor,
On her tippy toes as she stretches her petite frame,
Exhaling all the negative thoughts and energy.
She makes her way to her darkened bathroom.
She flips the switch, let there be light,
Her two hands come together to create a puddle of water,
The puddle kisses her face with refreshment.
Round two of the puddle, one more and she begins to stare.
She stares at herself in the mirror, drops of water leaving her face, free falling down to the sink.
She stares; wonder what she sees, perhaps she does not know.

Perhaps she sees a past she cannot escape,
A life she wants out of but doesn't know how to reinvent herself.
Her face reflects well, but her reflection of self-love is hazy.
Maybe she's just overreacting, that is just anxiety trying to be her breakfast.
She looks in the mirror, and tells that beautiful woman she sees, "I love you very much."
Today is a new day, and she will not let fear stand in her way.

How I Feel About Her (08/9/20 2:46 PM)

Tomorrow is not promised, but you are my today.
My open arms wrapped around you,
My chin landing on the surface of your skull.
The soft cushion of your hair smells of apples, oranges, and cream.
Give me your immaculate face,
Let me kiss you for hours and tell you I want more.
Have mercy on me, I miss you every time I blink.
Love is a mountain that you cannot fly over,
But you must climb.
I climbed to get your love, if I ever slip, then let me fall dangerously in love with you.
Meaningless dreams if I don't dream of you.
Your pulse is my paradise,
Your moisturized skin is escapism to my sins,
Your voice is my medicine of serenity,
Your knowledge is my cure to insanity.
Bless me with your presence,
Pull me in with your fragrance,
Then father me with your fertile womb.

"America is a land of stories that leaves out the truth."

A Mother's Pain (08/10/20 7:16 PM)

Close to fifty, she had five sons,
Never in her worst nightmare, did she think she'll lose any of them to cars, bullets and guns.
She gave birth through her womb, five times,
Four of her sons were not thugs, never committed a crime.
She had her oldest at sixteen, just a baby herself,
No help from the father, had to take care of him by herself.
The baby father was street struck,
Lost his life over fifty bucks.
She had crying contest with her newborn,
Holding him tight, this black curse is airborne.
Another man in her life now, she just had baby number two,
Looking at her baby's father, saying to him, "he looks just like you."
Six years later, he sticks around for a while, a father to his son and stepson,
He goes to the corner store and says, "just wait here on the steps son."
Drive-by out of the blue, his son's shirt covered in red,
Father runs out of the store, looks down the street, sees his son shot dead.
He drops his bags, he screams and runs to his son,
He calls her, crying, "our two sons have now become one."

She lost it; she went out of her mind,
Her youngest son is gone, if she could only turn back the time.
But the time kept moving forward, ten years,
Three more sons in the picture, but one son is
Missing, sporadic tears.
Her oldest joined the army, to serve his great nation,
She gets a knock on the door, a visit she dreaded, a visit of devastation.
"We regret to inform you," tragedy came back to her life,
Her heartbreak never healed, now her heart's being chopped with a knife.
She's in shock; how could this happen; how could this be?
She gave birth to five sons, that are now reduced to three.
Her mental health is beginning to deteriorate, she can't handle this pain,
She had to get away, she was going insane.
Ten years later; her three young sons are trying to maintain,
But they're street struck as well, driving in the fast lane.
The oldest of the 3 was riding a little too fast, in his friend's stolen car,
Terrible crash, her son didn't make it, but the friend survived with only a little scar.
The father doesn't want to tell her, she doesn't have a clue,

THE HEALING

She's been in the mental hospital for all these years; her five sons have now been tragically reduced to two.

He can't tell her this, if he does, she is done,

He can't tell her that they have lost another son.

He visits her, she asked, "how are our three wise men?"

But how can he tell her that one is no longer with us, and another is now serving life in the prison?

If he tells her the truth, she will grow ill and die,

He loves her too much, so he fed her the medication of lies.

She's lost, her brain is in another galaxy,

The pain won't let her come back to the world of reality.

She's in recess, they turn on the news, other patients are playing a game,

The news reported the car crash, she went absolutely insane,

She knew it was her son, because they mentioned his name.

They had to strap her in the bed, she couldn't do nothing but nod,

She lost another son, she lost her mind, and she lost her faith in God.

How could one mother go through so much,

If only she could see her sons, one more feel, just one last touch.

She has one son left, what will he do?

Will he survive, is he cursed? He doesn't have a clue.

He decided to go visit her, he has a gifted message for her now 50th birthday,
She's low on energy, she doesn't have much to say,
He says, "not to worry mom, I'll do all the talking okay?
I haven't been able to share this with dad, it's kind of difficult for me to say,
But I thought you should know, that I, I am gay."
She looks at him, speechless mouth, it doesn't move an inch,
They both just sit there, in the courtyard, on the bench.
He says again, "I'm gay mom, and I've known for a long time,
I hope I'm not hurting you, because hurting you would be the ultimate crime."
She looks at him with immaculate bliss,
Leans towards him, aims her lips at his cheek for a kiss.
Then another kiss, and another, and another,
She says to him, "I know you've suffered enough, with the loss of your brothers."
He says, "we've all been through it mom, especially you,"
She tells him, "thank you for visiting me on my birthday, to my last son I have left, I love you."
Before you judge her, call her crazy or insane,
Just know that you will never understand a mother's pain.

Naked Moon (08/10/20 1:06 PM)

I wondered why wolves would always howl at her,
Why animals always go crazy when she's in full nude.
She loves to be naked, glowing in the night,
She's been naked in the night for billions of years.
Once in a blue moon, she throws shade,
The shade of eclipse.
Many crater vaginas, yet she's a billion-year-old virgin.
What a tease she is, driving man wild,
As women leave men on "read,"
She leaves men on earth.

"Have you ever listened to Jill Scott after Midnight? A voice of soothing paradise. One of the most beautiful smiles your eyes will ever see.
She gives me healing."

Regret on A Train (08/11/20 5:39 AM)

He sits there, train screeching as it hits the breaks,
It comes to a stop, a stop at a regret he possibly makes.
Train door slides open, in she comes, then she sits,
His eyes never left her sight, playing a game on his phone, he had to press quit.
She sits across from him, so close in diameter, yet so far away from conversation,
He must make a move, say something before either reach their destination.
She looks at him for the first time, her face could replace the Mona Lisa,
What should he do? Ask for her name? Say, "hey let's get a slice of pizza?"
Yet he says nothing, back and forth they give each other smiles,
But his fear of rejection is so high, he's afraid to fall, he'll fall for miles.
The train has reached the last station, the ride has come to an end,
He can't lose her, this is his potential soulmate, his best friend.
She looks at him one last time, smiles and walks out the train,

A wet street of pouring rain drops, he'll give anything to take her hand, and they dance in the rain.

He finally decided in a split second to go for it and be brave,

He could never live with this regret; he refused to take this to the grave.

She waits for a taxi, no umbrella, her hair becomes frizzle,

He walks to her, puts his umbrella over their heads, protecting her from the heavy drizzle.

He looks at her, she says hello; her voice is the echo of paradise,

If love was a store, her kiss would be the ultimate merchandise.

He said to her, "if I didn't speak to you, I would have regretted it for the rest of my life,

Just to think I could be looking into the eyes of my future wife."

She smiles and says, "wow, I completely understand,

But I am so sorry, I already have a man."

His body was getting soaked, but his heart and brain were drained,

I guess these two will not be dancing in the rain.

God knows what he's doing, sooner or later it'll show,

When the right person comes for you, you'll feel it, you'll just know.

He'll be alright, he'll be okay,

At least he's not going home with a regret at the end of the day.

"One of the greatest bonds I've ever endured with women is when they would braid my hair. I felt like a king getting my Afro crown braided down".

He's Famous (0811/20 12:52 PM)

It's 3:17 in the morning, bad dreams in his brain,
He sees his best friend, his body's shaking, he feels the pain.
He wakes up half naked in a bed, with a group of women fully nude,
He crawls out of bed, lights a cigarette, he's not in the best mood.
He checks his social media, his concert was lit,
But he has his enemies, his tour bus took a fatal hit.
A spray of bullets hit the bus, someone wants him dead,
Security is a star's best friend; paranoia begins to spread.
His record sales are breaking records, the industry has found a new king,
Be he's not happy, not a game anymore, he doesn't trust anyone or anything.
Couldn't go back to sleep, a hard knock on the hotel room door,
He looks through the peep hole, it's his bodyguard from the tour.
He says, "boss we have to leave, downstairs there's already a mob of press,
He responded, "alright then, wait out here, just let me get dress."
He wakes the women up, tells them they have to leave,

Arguments are sparked, he should have given himself time to grieve.
The dream he had, of his best friend,
He was the one on the tour bus; a fantastic night meets a tragic end.
He comes out the lobby, early paparazzi gets the worm,
It was like walking through hell, had to move quickly, or he could burn.
Scrolling on his phone, #rip to his friend on every post,
The radio shows calling him a coward, social media trolls begin to roast.
He grows angry, people don't know the truth, they don't know the facts,
People saying, "he set his friend up," bullshit narrative, the whole crew was under attack.
He goes on his live; says every curse word known to man,
Tells people, "y'all wasn't there, stop with the lies, y'all never fucking understand.
He calls his "industry friends," but none accepted his calls,
He realized then, that in this industry, he has no friends at all.
He scrolls up the news feed as tears scrolls down his face,
He has to go to the police station; they must investigate this case.
He calls his attorney, he says, "I don't want to snitch,"

His attorney said, “do NOT say a word until I get there, don’t move your mouth, even if it itch.”
He now knows his truth, and being strong requires being alone,
He shuts down all his social media and throws down his phone.
This is the life he lives, just because he recorded some songs,
How does one gain the world, then everything goes completely wrong?
This lifestyle is fast, scary, and absolutely insane,
But this is the ultimate price to pay, in the wilderness of fortune and fame.

"Texting can be a very blunt, emotionless statement. That is why these "emojis" have become so popular, such a necessity to our dialogue online and through technology. Emojis give our conversations some seasoning and flavor. It gives some sensitivity and humanity."

A Mid-Life Blessing (08/12/20 12:46 PM)

She opens her door, lights on, an empty home,
A long day at work, kicks off her shoes, takes a peek at her phone.
No social media notifications, no text message, no date,
She's in for the night, she wonders if she'll ever find her soulmate.
In the last year of her forties, about to hit fifty years on this earth,
She's an aunt but not a mother, not once has she ever given birth.
Once upon her time, she was in love, maybe once or twice,
But the men she survived through; they were cruel, they weren't nice.
They did her so wrong, with their words and their fist,
She put a hold on love, started living her life, checking off her bucket list.
It's been years since a man has entered her heart,
Her father never was in her life, since the age of two, they were miles apart.
She calls her best friend, she verbally cries on her shoulder,
Her friend says, "go out and take a chance at love, you're not getting younger but older.
She knows her friend is absolutely right,

They both then decided to go out; a ladies night.

She meets her friend for dinner; their favorite diner,

As she arrives, her friend tells her, “girl, I just saw a man here, he couldn’t be any finer.”

She asked, “who, what, when, where?”

She turned around, there he was extremely handsome, freshly groomed with salt and pepper hair.

She turned to her friend and said, “giirrlllll you were RIGHT!”

When she saw him, it was like love at first sight.

Her friend says, “get up to use the bathroom, try to be seen,”

As she moves, she knocks over her glass bowl of ice cream,

Glass shatters, complete silence, now she’s made a scene.

But that caught the attention of him, he helps her clean the mess,

He cannot get over how beautiful she is in that sexy dress.

She greets him with a smile and says, “thank you so much,”

He says, “you’re welcome,” reached out his hand, like the ice cream, she melted from his touch.

His smile was her serenity, his eyes, his voice,

She says, “Dear God, please let him be the one, let him be the right choice.”

A chemistry is born; it is alive and well,

They both had a connection, hard to explain but it was there, they could tell.

THE HEALING

They exchanged their names, numbers, and availability,
He asked if he could see her tomorrow night, and she said,
"that's a definite possibility."
She goes back home, clicks on the lights,
She cannot wrap her brain around this miraculous night.
She pours her glass of wine and begins to drink,
Thoughts pour into her brain and she begins to think.
She thinks about this man, like wine, he aged well,
She's praying that he'll be her angel that heals her from a past of brutal hell.
A quick buzzing from her phone, lover boy is calling,
She's hesitant, she's scared, deliberately stalling.
In her mind she says, "what the hell," and answers saying, "hello?"
If only you could see her face, sipping her wine, listening to his voice, makes her mellow.
Time flies when you're having a good time,
Laying in her bed, talking with her possible, "partner in crime."
Conversation comes to an end, said their goodbyes, she hangs up her phone.
Tears with smiles, even though nothings set in stone,
This mid-life single woman is about to remedy being alone.

"Is love what we fairytale it to be, or is just a situation that two people put themselves in, blindly?"

She Was My Paradise (08/12/20 4:34 PM)

I've been through it all with her,
Her laughs, her moans, her cries, her anger.
I felt her skin pressed against mines,
Her skin as smooth as the wind blowing through open land.
Late nights of playing in her hair,
Entangled the knots that made her say, "ouch."
Sharing candy while we laid in bed,
One for her and one for me.
But the taste of her, tasted sweeter than any treat
Willy Wonka ever made.
Some mornings I would awaken before her,
To see her sleeping, to hear her breathing,
Unrecorded music to my ears.
Both of us wrapped in covers,
Naked like adult newborns.
My kiss to her was her alarm clock, different electricity,
Two pairs of eyes, one pair of lovers.
I loved when she said my name,
Heartbroken when she said goodbye.
I remember her, but I forgot her smell,
I forgot the sounds of her moans,
I miss her laughter and her voice.
I never saw her beautiful face ever again,

All I have are melted memories,

Frozen heartbreak, and a passionate kiss

That has yet to be replaced.

My eyes bleed of tears,

Emotional thoughts at war with

my appreciation to have known her,

To love her the way I did.

I pray that I can find a replacement,

No, I pray that I can love again, more than I ever loved her.

Reality is too real sometimes.

She was my reality,

She was my fantasy,

She was my best friend,

She was my paradise.

The Good Cop (08/12/20 5:20 PM)

He wakes up at dawn, on his couch, didn't make it to his bed,
He goes to his bedroom, sleeping wife, gives a kiss to her head.
In the shower he goes, more thoughts in his mind than the drops of water,
He dries off, gets dressed, checks on his son and daughter.
He wanted to start his day early, a very special day for this man,
For this is his last day on duty, retiring after an 18-year span.
He's driving around, reminiscing about all he's been through, all he's seen,
The crimes he's solved, criminals and all, the streets were ever so mean.
All the riots and protests, he saw people loot,
A bittersweet feeling that this is his final day wearing that blue suit.
He lost his partner some years ago,
He always keeps him in his memories, no matter where he goes,
The neighborhood kids love him, he's their favorite superhero.
One time he saved an infant child from a burning car,
Years later he saved his drowning son, performing CPR.

It's been a hell of a ride, can't say it's been all fun,
He's just very grateful that he rarely had to draw and fire his gun.
Sitting in his squad car, his eyes grow teary and moist,
Calling up the dispatcher, for this will be the final time they hear his voice.
His peers, his brothers and sisters overwhelm him with love, praises, and prayer,
A colossal party awaits him tonight; all invited, including the Mayor.
His emotional voice says, "it has been an honor serving my community; my country of the red, white, and blue,
I love you all, take care, God bless, 10-42."

Interlude

The Healing

So, how are you feeling so far? I hope at this point in the book, you have found yourself in some of these poems, in some of these stories. I will say that some of them are fictional, they do not entirely represent my personal life experiences. Most of these works come from my mind. Well, I will also say they come from God. I would just think a lot, brainstorming about situations or events that go on in the world, things I have barred witness to in the past, and I just begin to write them down. I begin to tell these stories as they go. I start off with a sentence, then that sentence just guides me through the journey, and I let the poem write itself.

I find writing to be very therapeutic for me. Once I get started, I do not stop. I love where the story goes. The thoughts, the ideas in my mind, they just come from above somewhere. Perhaps from spirits who lived in another lifetime, who shares their stories with me, who channels into my mind, and I just become a vessel; an instrument who writes their stories for them. I do believe that, I believe that my work is universally influenced by what I see, and what I do not see. It is influenced by what I think, what I feel, and what I believe.

I just take all of my love, my hate, if there is any; I take all of my pain, my joy, my pleasure, fantasies and desires, and I create these bodies of work. I must admit, sometimes, after I finished a poem, then after I finish proofreading it, I say to myself, "Wow, where did that come from?" I would just ask myself that question when I write a poem, and how it just falls into place.

Writing is my official form of healing. Whenever I feel anything, I just write about it. Whether it is a poem, short stories, I just write. This is my way of healing. That is why I named this book, and this interlude, "*The Healing*." I want you, the reader, to find your healing. What do you do in your life that gives you healing? Do you write as well? Do go out somewhere and just clear your head? Do you visit friends and family, and spend some quality time with them?

Perhaps you came to this book, to find some healing. To find some peace, comfort, and some understanding. As I mentioned in the introduction, I was taking a different direction with my third book. I was going to tell a story about my life experiences, my opinions on America and how I feel about it in today's world. But I felt that now was not the right time for such a book. Now is the time for some recovery, and some healing.

It is time for people to clear their minds of the toxic energy that surrounds them. The polluted atmosphere they are living in. Whether you are dealing with heartbreak, pain, trauma, or a breakup. I want you to know that life will always be worth living. It will not always be fair, but it is definitely worth living. What did I write on the back cover of this book? I wrote, "*The pain will win some battles, but love will always win the war.*"

Do not let pain be your whole life. The loss of a loved one, your wound may not heal completely; especially when the loss is so sudden. But I do believe that the reason why the wound never heals, is because we place the blame on ourselves, why that loved one is gone. We feel that if we could have just stopped that person from going out, from getting on that motorcycle, or in that car. Whatever the situation was, we may feel that we could have stopped them and saved their life. That is why our wounds never fully heal; we place some blame on ourselves, and that keeps the pain healthy and sustainable in our lives.

Let me tell you something, we have to let go. I say we, because I am also someone who has to work on letting go. I practice what I preach. We have to let go of the pain that prevents us from moving forward with our lives. Stop putting the blame on yourself or the other person, for why the relationship did not work out. Even if two people are nice human beings, that does not mean that they will have a healthy relationship together. That might actually be the most toxic. Because both may try to outdo each other's acts of kindness, and over time they grow bored of one another, then one cheats, and then comes the madness.

We have to let go of our, "should of, could of, would of," mentality, and move forward in a direction that distance us away from the past. Because if there is one thing I have learned about the past, the past does not stay in the past. The past moves forward, and that is why the past always catches up to us. If the past catches up, the past can repeat itself.

You know that saying, "history can repeat itself," well that is because people do not know how to let go of certain situations, move forward in their lives, and find their healing.

That is why when I see how America is making these changes, changing their symbols, removing statues and confederate flags across the nation. I find that to be a good thing, but not exactly the ultimate task at hand. The way I look at it; this whole removal of the statues and confederate flags, this reminds me of a time, when the dream team went to O.J. Simpson's house to remove all the photographs he took with his Caucasian friends, and they replaced those photos with other photos of O.J. with African American friends and family. Placing up African artifacts, to give his home some "blackness." To convince the jury, who were majority African American jurors, that he was for his people, African American people, that he represented his people, and loved his people to the fullest. However, that was not the case back then, and I do not believe that is the case today. It was not the truth.

Today we see "Black Lives Matter" on basketball courts and jerseys, and I guess that is supposed to impress African American people? It does not really impress me at all; I just see it all as a farced, lucrative symbol that makes for a good photo opportunity, and it will not change what needs to be changed.

What must be done is removing the statue of thought, of white supremacy. People who believe they are superior, who are above other ethnic groups of people, that is a thought that has not been replaced, changed, or has left people's mentality. Their minds are set in stone, like a statue, and that should be the real focus; changing people's ways of thinking about other people. How about removing those statues? The statues of racist thoughts in people's minds.

I'm sure by now, many of you have seen the sickening events of the youth ranting and raving on TikTok, all the racist videos you have probably witnessed. Their minds are accumulating those statues of thought. Once those thoughts are set in stone, locked in people's minds, it will be extremely difficult to have them removed.

Now, of course I am not spreading an assumption that all Caucasian people are racist, absolutely not. However, I feel that it is necessary to inform all Caucasian people, to understand that not all African American people are criminals, thugs, ignorant, or unreliable people. Not all Latinos are gun and drug trafficking people; we are some very well read, well educated human beings. We will always have our differences in how we live our lives and raise our children. But our differences should never be depicted as weapons that we use to attack each other.

As you can see, I used the terms "Caucasian and African American." I did not use the terms "Black and White." Now before I say what I am going to say, I already know many will disagree. But this is my book, my voice, and I will stand by my opinion, unapologetically. The terms of "black people" and "white people;" one day, people will have to remove these terms from how we identify ourselves. I know that this will not happen in our lifetime. But for the people of the future, to remove the stigmas and stereotypes of "black and white," and refer to ourselves as just African American and Caucasian people, I believe that will one day be the healing that we need to put an end to our prejudices against ourselves.

Why do I say all of this? Well, if you look at the definitions of the words black and white, you will understand why we as people, have such a misunderstanding among ourselves. When I looked up the definitions of "white," it said, "*auspicious or fortunate, morally pure; innocent, without malice; harmless*." Then when I looked up the definitions of the word "black," it said, "*soiled or stained with dirt, deliberately harmful, hostile, threatening, evil, wicked, and without any moral quality or goodness*."

My God; are you kidding me? None of those definitions define me at all. Also, when you think about it, you hear the terms, "black balled, blackmail, blacklisted, black magic, black market, or even wearing black clothing at a funeral." Also, when a black cat crosses your path, you were told they bring bad luck, or it is a curse. Not to mention the mockery of "blackface." All of these terms are a toxic, despicably negative label. So, when you take the definition of the word "black" and place that word in front of "people," and then you have "black people," how can you possibly expect anyone to respect, care about, or love a black person? Even other "black" people for that matter? When a "black" person walks into a store, whoever the owner is of that store, they already have that definition programmed in their brains, that this human being, this "black" person, is indeed hostile, a criminal, wicked, evil, and without any morals or goodness in their heart.

But let that person be "white;" the pure, innocent, harmless person; they will be treated with immaculate bliss, superiority even. As if an angel walked into the store. Let me tell you, I unfortunately have come across some "white" people, who were not as innocent, pure, or harmless. The proof is in the pudding, we see videos every single day. But the programming in our minds, has us believing that "white is right," and "black is coming to attack." By the way, this is nothing new. I am not exactly telling you, the reader, anything new that was just discovered and is reaching the surface of America. These stereotypes and stigmas have been trained and conditioned in our society for centuries. Not only in the minds of the American people, but in people all over the world. That is why, me personally, the phrase "Black Lives Matter," I do not believe it is going to stand the test of time. We see it already; people from other ethnic backgrounds, who are using the phrase for their own personal agenda.

My personal opinion, as long as we accept the definition of us as "black" people, our lives will never be treated with respect. We will always be looked upon as evil, wicked, trouble making criminals. We will always be at the bottom of the barrel. When I look at the definitions for the word "black;" they do not define me, as a man, as a human being. They do not define me at all. I am the opposite of all of those definitions. I absolutely resent them completely.

So, what am I saying to you? What I am saying is and brace yourself; I will not ever define myself as a "black" person. I am escaping that stigmatic stereotype that has cursed African Americans since day one, and still is a curse upon us to this day. Now, am I saying that I define myself as a "white" person? No, absolutely not. I am not a color. I am man, a human being, who is of African descent. From now on, that is how I identify myself, on this earth. Also, to be fair, I will no longer identify Caucasian people as "white." You are not a color either.

Think about it, there are Asians, Latinos, Middle Eastern, but when it comes to Europeans and Africans; we call ourselves, "black and white." Hundreds of thousands of years of human evolution, has been tragically corrupted and reduced to "black and white." A history of false narratives and unproper identification.

Now, I understand our history of "the Black Panther Party, the Black Power movement, black owned businesses, and Black History Month." I understand that many African American people who might read this and will completely disagree with me. I understand; there is just too much history imbedded in the terms "black," or "blackness." That is why I said that one day, people of the future, may have to follow through with this idea of how to morally identify themselves. By no means am I saying that we as African Americans should forget or deny black history. We must absolutely learn from it. However, we should archive our identity as "black" people and move forward to our proper identity; which is people of African descent. I feel the same way about archiving the term of "white" people.

With all of that being said, think about it. Do we really want to go our whole existence being identified as a color? A color of ill definition? A definition that prevents us from ever achieving our truest potential? I showed you the definition of the word, “black.” As of today, I have absolutely no problem identifying as a man of African descent. But I will no longer accept or address myself as “black,” nor will I address other African American people as “black” people.

Oh, I understand that I may receive a lot of “blacklash,” as they say on twitter. I have prepared myself for that, by removing myself from social media completely. But you must understand, I am speaking for myself, and not for every other African American person. Even though you may disagree with me, all I ask is that you think about it. You do not have to change your mind, but we as African American and Caucasian people, we have to remove these false, corrupt narratives from our psyche. I will speak more about this later. But we all need to recover and heal from this “Black and White” war before we kill our truest definition and purpose of humanity.

I know you were probably not expecting any of this in a poetry book, did you? Well, hopefully it makes some sense to you. Maybe it won’t today, but someday. But anyways, to wrap up this interlude, I want to say that healing does not happen overnight. It does not happen with one post or tweet. You must figure out what is causing you such pain and remove yourself from it; whether that be a person, place, or thing.

To heal, you must change yourself. Sometimes you must remove people from your life, change your job, or simply change your hobbies. Find a new hobby for yourself. I am sure for some; a new hobby is reading books. Perhaps for you the reader, this is the first book you picked up a long time. If that is to be true, I hope you were able to find yourself somewhere in these poems and stories, and that you were able to have some healing.

Speaking of healing, I have started you off with a poem, self-titled, "*The Healing*." I do not know if you are going through something at the moment. I do not know if life is stressing you out; I would say that during this Covid-19 pandemic, we are all going through our struggles. So, as you continue reading the second half of this book, I hope you are enjoying what you have read so far. Hopefully you find it entertaining, and you found a little of yourself, somewhere in these poems, and these stories. So, let us begin, the second half, "*The Healing*."

The Healing (07/26/20 4:10 PM)

Close the lids of your eyes,

Forget what people have to say, ignore the lies.

You are not crazy, just in a crazy world, a bizarre space,

Don't be afraid to look in the mirror, look at that beautiful face.

Put the phones away; in time, your mind and spirit will heal,

Human connections are declining, we can't touch, we can't feel.

Take a look at the sky, forget all your heartbreak,

Don't torture yourself with reminiscing tears, how much more can you take?

They can't hurt you anymore, your heart is pure,

Dismiss the pain from your gut; your spirit will heal for sure.

Mental health is everything, don't feed the stress,

Count your blessings, not your money; nothing more, nothing less.

Say hello to people, cost you nothing, it's free,

They say hello right back, the power of a smile, you see?

Don't be hard on yourself, people do love you,

Stand up for yourself when disrespected; no one's above you.

Secrets in your mind, never tell who you don't trust,

Secrets so old, they began to rust.

Life is worth living; be still-minded and let it find you,

All positivity from here on out, even if people are unkind to you.
Give yourself purpose, direction, and meaning,
Heal your spirit; your mind and body will do the cleaning.
The healing; thank yourself later in the mirror, you just may cry,
Oh, before you go, a plant-based diet will never hurt to try.

An Unborn Call to Momma (08/13/20 6:46 PM)

The waiting room she sits, she waits,
Her appointment was a half hour ago, her doctor is running late.
A little longer she waits, her eyelids slide down, she catches invisible Z's,
She dreams of her unborn baby, it cries saying, "momma, save me please!"
The dream ended too quickly, she jumps out of her sleep,
She's filled with emotion, thinking about her unborn baby, she silently begins to weep.
Saying to herself, "what the hell am I doing, I have to leave,"
She doesn't want to live with these regrets, an everlasting marriage to grieve.
The door opens, the assistant says, "we're ready for you miss,"
She cannot believe she's telling her unborn child, "you are dismissed."
Her eyes give birth to newborn tears,
In her mind, "Momma save me please," is all she hears.
She lays there on the bench, teary eyes staring at the ceiling,
She can't follow through with this, she must go and find some healing.

The doctor comes in, her heart's racing, but can't cross this finish line,
She's thinking, "is this murder under God's crime?"
She's still looking at the ceiling, the doctor says, "you are absolutely sure about this, right?"
She responded, "no, I want my child to come through my tunnel, to be born and see the light."
The doctor said, "absolutely, this is your choice,
She just broke down; she couldn't stop hearing her unborn child's voice.
As she gets dress, she looks in the mirror,
She prays to God, hoping that he hears her.
She cries, "I'm so sorry, I'm so sorry, please forgive me,
I know now that this life growing in my womb, is a blessing within me.
She saved her unborn child, a mother she shall be,
Where's the father you may be thinking? Well, Welcome to 2020.

You're Beautiful Regardless (08/13/20 9:24 PM)

She looks in her mirror, judges her face,
There are things she wants to fix, things to replace.
She wants a thinner nose, fuller lips,
Bigger breast, butt and thighs, she'll kill for shapely hips.
The doctor is her new boyfriend, she has more appointments than dates,
Spending thousands and thousands, I can't imagine, insurance and rates.
Insecurities and low self-esteem,
Doing all of this for what? Instagram it seems.
Self-paparazzi is her self-destruction,
Thousands of blueprint photos, plotting her reconstruction.
Perfection on the tip of their tongue, desperate to take a lick,
30-50 selfie angles to choose from, hard to take her pick.
Anxiety injected in her brain, ugly procedures for pretty results,
Is beauty the new God? A new religion, or occult?
She had more surgery, she gained more followers,
She loves the compliments from random strangers who follows her.
You're beautiful regardless, no need for a swollen body,
It is not your fault; you're living in such a judgmental society.
The knife is not your friend, all this money you spend,

Botched nose, acting like nobody knows, people try hard to pretend.
Wounded faces healing for beauty,
Surgical procedures gone wrong, crying to their doctors and they say, “so sue me.”
They’re getting younger and younger, their face has not even matured,
She’s a baby, so much life to live, so much to explore.
Beauty and perfection have mentally enslaved them, the word ugly must die,
They see that word in their comments, a light word that causes heavy cries.
You’re beautiful regardless, but the choice is yours to call,
Oh, if I could be your mirror, mirror on the wall,
I would say, “you are so beautiful, change nothing at all.”

The Eighties (08/15/20 1:12 AM)

Oh, the nylon lights on Miami vice,

Crockett's theme sounds so nice.

Daniel-San; wax on, wax off,

Reganomics; tax on, tax off.

Business got risky, just ask Tom Cruise,

The crash of 87,'please no more bad news.

You can walk the walk,

But can you "*Talk Talk*?"

The curse of crack cocaine, turned people into zombies like thriller,

HIV and AIDS; I hate to bring it up; it was a serial killer.

Number 23 was making his mark in the Windy City,

Tyson put more men on a canvas than a painter, he showed no pity.

There was something about this era, the classic video games and toys,

How about those thirsty vampires from *Fright Night* and *The Lost Boys*?

I miss Corey Haim, an icon for sure,

In Minnesota, when it purple rains, it pours.

Warhol meets Basquiat, the art world was never the same,

Blondie rapping, Madonna vogues, Nintendo says, "let's play a game."

There were brass knuckles and knives,
Punches and stab wounds, people fighting for their lives.
Jerry Rice dominated, could catch anything at will,
Like Kate Bush, he was always running up that hill.
We'll never get this kind of music again; it's one of a kind,
Forgive me for the obsession, my appreciation for this era goes beyond my mind.
Maybe I am just obsessed with the art, but ignore the reality, the pain,
Still listen to Fab 5 Freddy and Big Daddy Kane?
Some may think I'm crazy, oh so lonely,
Don't judge me if you don't Klaus Nomi.
The famous Air Jordan's and shell toes,
High tops; Track suits were the go-to clothes.
MJ doing the moonwalk, wish I had a ticket,
The DeBarge family, oh I like it.
Go back and study the eighties, give it a chance,
Listen to David Bowie's "*Let's Dance*."
Billy Idol, Bryan Adams, Mummy Calls, heard it all,
Graffiti on the trains, bridges, and brick walls.
I can't really claim the eighties, I can't say it's mine,
But I'm grateful I had a taste of it, I was born in 89.'

Rose in A Bottle

(08/15/20 3:04 PM)

My footprints in the sand, yours are missing,
I miss your hand I used to hold, the hugs, all the kissing.
A sunset to remember, still waters of the ocean,
I didn't mean all those things, I'm sorry for the unnecessary emotion.
The words I launched at you, hurt you so much,
The verbal daggers to your brain; God I miss your touch.
I guess I didn't deserve you, even when I earned your trust,
So many accusations, manipulation in your mind, our love immaturely failed to lust.
We were tight like shoelace knots, but I could never walk in your shoes,
I took your shoes for granted, I gambled and thought I couldn't lose.
Two dozen roses in your hands, they meet my face,
You walked out of the room, leaving roses all over the place.
You didn't even say goodbye,
Tears to water every rose, as I begin to cry.
All except one; this rose was oh so delicate,
It was the only pink rose, as pink as a pelican.
A representation of our innocence, happiness; for you to be my wife,
Now you leave me, on our anniversary, just out of my life?

So here I am, a rose in a bottle, standing in the wet sand,
Staring at the ocean, with the bottle in my right hand.
I look at the bottle, I look at the rose,
My love for you will never die, but sadly, it will never grow.
I baptized the bottle in the ocean waters, it floated away,
Even though our love has reached its destination, I know I'll be okay.
I stretched the curves of my mouth up, created a smile as the bottle sails far into the sea,
A moment in time, that I thought would last forever, but it just wasn't meant to be.

Penitentiary Blues (08/15/20 10:24 PM)

He's been innocent for seven years,
Convicted; he didn't remain silent, the lies they fed his ears.
Correctional officer walking passed his cell,
It's hard to remain an innocent angel while you're imprisoned in hell.
23 hours of concrete walls, no birds or grass,
Tears for his momma as he talks to her, through a plate glass.
He tells her, "get me out of here, I want to go home,"
She says, "we're trying our best, but your case is 85% set in stone."
All this time on his hands, book after book he reads,
No crime committed with his hands, framed solicitation; not his bricks of weed.
Judge said no bail, keep him in jail,
No room for fairytales, just nightmares and spells,
Christmas comes, Christmas goes; no Christmas carols, or jingle bells.
Laying in his bed, staring at the ceiling,
These last seven years, he's been finding some healing.
He bled through those years,
His wounds crying bloody tears,
He's soon to be released, hallelujah cheers.
His cell opens and closes for one last time,

Was robbed of his time but will continue to rise as he climbs.
He collects his past belongings, speed walks out the door,
He hopes he'll never have to step foot in this hell in a cell environment anymore.
He's through the exit, lifts his head up to the sky,
He took a deep breath, and exhaled, with closed eyes.
His family waits for him after this now eight-year bid,
His mother, his sister, his brothers, and his now 8-year-old kid.
He hugs his son, tells him, "I know now I may be a stranger to you,
But we'll get through this, and no matter what, I'll always love you."

Smartphones (08/16/20. 6:20 PM)

Scroll, scroll, scroll your thumb, gently up the screen,
Merrily, Merrily, Merrily, Merrily, life is but a stream.
Streaming friendships, relationships, and politics it seems,
They're everywhere, even in our dreams.
Notifications in the middle of the night,
Tapping letters on these screens; billions of Vanna White.
People saying, "don't call, text me only,"
Send a text, left on read, damn this world's so phony.
These six-inch screens own us, they have us hooked,
Don't believe me? When was the last time you picked up a book?
Selfies on the go, shot from different angles,
Racist cop being recorded, what's up with the arm and knee strangles?
Living in this heads down, likes up world; hold up, let me tweet that,
Damn she hot, swipe to the right, I want to meet and greet that,
"Oh, sorry I can't meet up, it's a long story; but not longer than the stories of her partying on Snapchat.
Oh my God, low battery, running to an outlet like a sprinter,
Smartphones are a way of life; the new five percenters.
Algorithms are in order, don't get mad, get ads,

Perfumes consumed, doom and gloom, they take advantage of the gullible and sad.
People screaming at their phones, let's talk on FaceTime?
People record everything, the most brutal, deadliest crimes.
Protect your secrets and data, don't lack,
Bad actors create duplicate profiles, they love to hack.
Addictive games, @ names, nosey eyes can't focus on their lanes,
Purchased a ticket on an app; buses, trains, and planes.
Texting your friend on the phone saying, "lol, you're always late,"
Can't have a date without the phone being next to the dinner plate,
Wait, got to snap a shot for the gram, #itwasgreat,
Notifications and emails saying, "if you enjoyed this, give us a five-star rate."
Have you ever left your house without your phone?
Lose your phone, you lose your mind, like the terminator, it's now our mechanical backbone.
Give a smartphone to a baby, baby stops crying,
Give it to adults, they'll record people dying.
Hey Siri; oops, sorry! It knows our voice, knows our name,
Card numbers and photos by the thousands, smartphones changed the game.
Every five minutes, you just have to take a look,

You still don't believe me do you? I bet you're reading this on your phone, the e-book.

That's okay; when there's an iPhone there's a way,

These are just tools at the end of the day.

Use them, do not let them use you,

Antonio Meucci; how could we thank you?

Some of you are probably thinking right now, "wait, who?"

"Politicians are promise makers but not promise keepers."

Lust for Many,

Love for One (08/16/20 9:26 PM)

No one man should have all these women,
But he did, and he wanted more of them.
Until that one diamond in the rough came into his life,
He knew she was the one, she gave birth to his idea of being his wife.
Many girlfriends sliding in his DM's,
So many delicious candies, they came in every color like M&M's.
But there was something about this one, she was special, unique,
She was like a single from a triple album, she stood out, she leaked.
He stepped to her, she looked him up and down,
She said, "I heard about you, I heard you like to get around."
He said, "yea well don't believe everything you hear, some women will lie just to keep me,"
She responded, "yea, yea, yea; so why do you want to speak with me?"
He gave her his million-dollar smile, an expert at his game, he's a pro,

She curved him like a comma four times, gave him that trillion-dollar NO.
He's not used to rejection, "yes women" all over the place,
But he's not giving up on her, he loves this thrill, loves the chase.
If only you could see her, they'd actually make a cute pair,
Five feet six inches, dark brown curly hair,
Erykah Badu type of eyes; careful, don't stare.
He handed her his phone, asked for her number and name,
She said, "boy bye, I'm not about to be another player in your game."
He said, "what do mean? I'm dead serious, no cap,"
She gave in and began to press those numbers; tap, tap; tap, tap.
He tells her to save it in his contacts,
Looking in her eyes, asking if they're contacts,
She looked at him with sass and said, "boy, ain't nothing fake on me," then gives his phone back.
He said, "alright cool, but keep in mind, I'm a man not a boy,"
She said, "okay MAN, but you keep in mind, I'm woman and not a toy."
His eyebrows went up on that response; she put him in check,
He knows she is not the one to tolerate any disrespect.
They say their good nights, and go their separate ways,

Some time goes passed, just a couple days.
He's hesitant to be the one reaching out first,
What a complex; he doesn't want to come off that he's dying of thirst.
He says, "what the hell," text her saying, "good morning, how are you?"
Sitting back waiting for her to reply, time goes by, it's now five after two.
No word from her, not even an emoji,
Anxiously waiting, he checks his IG.
He looks up her name, her profile is set to private,
"DAMN!!" His frustrations grow, she's hard to get.
His thirsty drools over her, he's like a desperate hound dog,
I think he's met his match, maybe he no longer wants to be a dog.
His phone begins to ring, but it wasn't her, it was "just a friend,"
They exchanged a few words, he told her, "I've met someone, our "situationship" has come to an end."
One by one, he duplicates this message to all of them,
To Dana, Cassandra, Latifah, Briana, the other Latifah, and Kim.
It's almost eight o'clock at night, still she hasn't responded a word,
He's mad now, he dismissed all his little birds,

Now he's saying, "man, this shit is for the birds."
Finally, he received a call in the middle of the night,
It was her saying, "I'm so sorry I wasn't able to get to you, I had a very long flight."
Who would have thought she was actually on an electronic bird,
He almost forgot; she has the sexiest voice he's ever heard.
He said, "oh wow, that's okay, didn't know you were planning a getaway,"
She said, "oh no, I'm a flight attendant, I travel almost every other day."
He's surprised by her, not your average girl,
He begins a long conversation with her; she's very intelligent, and she's traveled around the world.
Static in his phone, he asked, "what's that sound?"
She said, "oh sorry, I just exited out the plane, we just landed on the ground."
She then said, "so MAN, if you want to seriously see me again, here are my rules,"
He grabs his pen and paper and says, "oh, name them; I'm just a water hose in your lawn, trying to get you wet like a pool."
She said, "ahh, what the hell did you just say?"
He said, "oh, I'm sorry, I'm sorry; it was a bad joke, okay?"

THE HEALING

Her rules, she slowly said, "*respect my body, it's not a punching bag,*
My ex thought it was; by my hair he pulled and dragged.
Don't ever call me a bitch, I hate that word so much,
He called me that every day, he was never gentle, such a raping touch.
I told you I'm a woman, not your toy,
He put me through hell, even caused me to miscarry my baby boy.
I thought he was going to kill me, I thought I was going to die,
I said the only way he'll never hurt me again, is if I escape, thousands of feet in the sky."
Tears free falling from his face as he hears her story,
He realized that this is a strong, brave woman who survived; God be the glory.
He tells her, "you have my word, I will never harm a curly brown hair on your head,
But if only I could put my hands your ex, he'd be dead."
Her trillion-dollar NO, became a priceless okay,
They planned a date; she comes back in a couple of days.
She likes him, he likes her; she's like his angel, literally flying up above,
He thanks God for bringing her into his life, no more lust; for her, it'll be true love.

"Progress is not just about the removal of tainted historical imagery, but the removal of tainted thinking so history does not repeat itself."

I Appreciate You (08/17/20 4:12 PM)

I open my eyes, turn my head, I see you,
No mistress, no third parties, just me and you.
I gently caress your gracious cheek, your flawless face,
A Mona Lisa in bed with me, a painting I could never replace.
You open your hazel iris, we have childish staring contest,
Breakfast in bed for you today, what is your special request?
A makeup free face, wrapped in covers,
If you ever leave me, it'll be difficult, but I'll recover.
But I won't think that; you're here, you're real,
I never met a woman like you before, I can't explain the way you make me feel.
You're my amusement when I have time to kill,
You're my pain killer, when I need help to heal,
You fulfill my hunger with the most delicious meals,
You're my serenity, my calm before the storm, my peace be still.
I press my back against the wall, while I watch you sleep,
I hope you're dreaming of me, while you're counting sheep,
I'm so grateful and blessed, you're so beautiful, my God I could just weep.
I say all of that to simply say this,

I love you; from the way you walk, the way you talk, and the way you kiss,
Every time I blink in your presence, that is a split second of you that I sincerely miss.
Do I love you too much? I don't know, I don't care,
I love taking selfies in the mirror with you, a reflection of an inseparable pair.
You're my favorite roommate, my soulmate,
More kisses than I can even calculate.
It all began with a blind date with you,
We became best friends, a night so great with you,
Chemistry; so much that I can relate to you,
As I curve your hair behind your ear, I whisper and say,
"I appreciate you."

Call It What You Want (08/17/20 9:16 PM)

Thugs, drugs, hugs, slugs, too young for cemetery bugs.
Hip hop, guns pop, slain rappers' albums reach the top.
Political game, capital gains, citizens in pain.
Judges, grudges, no budgets, no traveling luggage.
Wars, the poor, the wounds, the gore and sores.
Screams, dreams, live streams, addictive screens.
The killings, oil spilling, no feelings, where's the healing?
Where's Marley, where's Pac, where's Lennon, wish we could push back the clock.
Why Nipsey, why Gianna and Kobe, why the others, please hold me.
The threats, the last breaths, the deaths, the everlasting regrets.
The tears, the fear, can't believe everything you hear.
Reality is a trip that we didn't choose to fall in,
You don't have a face mask? You're not getting in the mall then.
Black and white; tainted formula of a cultural Armageddon,
Wars of complexion are the devil's resurrection, murder by a knee and arm again and again.
Bullets don't love us; why they have a special place in people's hearts?
Cupid gone wild, guns replaced his arrows and darts.

America has more debt than there are galaxies, look at how much we spent,
We're broke not bent, nickel and dime hustling, but our dollar isn't worth a cent.
Curses, no churches, coughing into coffins,
Cancer no answers,
Broadway actors and Dancers,
No tickets; shows cancelled.
Putting on a smile is like a 7-day trail,
Trail ended; now it's sadness every month; subscribed in denial.
Lord have mercy; mercy, mercy we,
Natural deforestation; suicidal trees.
They're tired, hurricanes ripping them from their roots,
If trees could talk, some would say, "I suffered from strange fruit."

Strange Land (08/17/20 10:38 PM)

Shackles on their feet and hands,
Speaking a language, they didn't understand.
Seasick by an unsolicited evil cruise,
Dark skin, a darker bruise.
Tossed into the ocean, dead before they drowned,
Hurricanes followed the path of the ships; they never start on the ground.
Brains contained in fear; barracoons and whips,
Turn men and women into slaves, more slaves, more ships.
Darkness for months, the clinging of iron chains,
Mental enslavement; how much fear can you put in one's brain?
Others chose to breathe under water than to serve another,
They were mothers, fathers, sons, brothers.
Heads down, don't look at master,
Can't run, can't escape, their whips and bullets were much faster.
A Momma sold for silver and gold,
No questions asked, you do what you're told,
Rebellious spirits, fearless and bold.
Slashing the flesh; over and over,
But they didn't give in, they grew bolder and bolder.
Sickening Incest forced; a son breeds with his mother,

Breeding for bigger slaves, his son is also his brother.
Picking thorns out of their hands as they pick cotton,
Blood stains, profit gains, feeding them meat that was spoiled and rotten.
A thick line between the house and the field,
We'll never know exactly how many were killed.
Trees were meant for birds nesting, and hearing the sounds of the leaves,
But they used them for a horror you couldn't imagine, you'd never believe.
Strange fruits; nooses are the wicked stem,
Castrations and amputations; feet, toes, limb from limb.
More bloodshed than a quill bled,
Salt in the slashing; too late, the horses ripped them to shreds.
Children's eyes saw hell on earth,
Made to feel they were slaves since birth.
Then there was the birth of Nat turner and Araminta Ross,
She changed her name, Harriet Tubman became a leader, a boss.
It doesn't take money to free the poor,
If only they knew they weren't slaves, she could have saved more.
The Civil War; the North versus the South,
Juneteenth was a miracle; master placed a pistol in his mouth.

You can't find 13 on a clock, just an amendment to the constitution,
Layers of laws, convicted, no need for prosecution.
Life imprisonment; from the boats, to the fields, to the bars, to the grave,
The mind; oh, the mind is such a terrible thing to enslave.
Here we are, trying to survive on this strange land,
Silence, you here that? It's our ancestors saying, "*why are you killing each other? We just don't fucking understand*!"

"Marriage is like a manager; love is the superstar. We as people are just super fans of love."

The Imperfect Woman (08/18/20 12:15 AM)

I met a woman; I looked at her, but didn't stare,
I couldn't help how attractive she was with gray strains of hair.
Her teeth were somewhat crooked, she did love to smoke,
But she could always make me laugh with her effortless timing of jokes.
A different complexion but we had a special connection,
She had wisdom, charisma, loved showing affection.
I guess I enjoyed her imperfections, something about her was truly beautiful,
A nomadic personality; I love how she viewed the world.
She looks me in the eyes, her undivided attention is incredible,
Her defined profile as she turns her head, blows out smoke, simply unforgettable.
She wasn't rich by paper, but wealthy by life,
She made many points, sharper than Michael Myers knife.
She told me her story; what a journey, what a tale,
She once said to me, "never be afraid to fail."
You live and you learn, from her I learned a lot,
She looks great for her age, a mother she is not.
I asked her what the secrets to life are, she said there's none,
Just stay safe, live life, have more fun.

That was it, she had the answer,

She was a warrior, survived her battle with cancer.

I found beauty in an imperfect woman; how could this be?

Now I understand that beauty is not just about what you see,

Beauty lies within her, within you, within me.

Three Birds and A Gummy (08/18/20 6:00 AM)

Waiting for the bus, running late I see,

I saw three birds on the ground, picking at a worm made of gummy.

I wonder if they knew, knew the difference of a gummy and a real one,

Perhaps they did, wasn't expecting it to be a sweet one.

Picking away at the sugar-coated worm, I still wondered if they were confused,

A worm is a worm, perhaps they didn't care, you can't beg and choose.

Quite hysterical watching them enjoy this worm of yellow and green,

Too bad I didn't record it, that would have been a memorable scene.

But I do remember it, this is a memory in my mind,

This memory is a special one; it's one of a kind.

The last thing I remember of the three birds and the gummy worm,

One of the birds pick it up with its beck, flew away, and never returned.

“Be careful with media; it could make you feel sorrier for the rich more than you feel sorry for the poor.”

Father and Son (08/18/20 6:30 PM)

Father: Hey, I wanted to see you, I'm glad you're here,

Son: Hi, yea, no problem; I saw your message and I was near.

F: So, first thing I want to say is I'm sorry for what I said to you the other night,

S: Yea, I'm sorry too; didn't expect it to turn into a horrific fist fight.

F: You know, your grandfather and I had a similar altercation, God rest his soul,

S: I remember you telling me. You said after that fight, he got drunk and crashed into one of those streetlight poles.

F: Yea, I didn't even get a chance to say I'm sorry, or goodbye,

S: But it wasn't your fault, no one would think that right after a fight, someone would die.

F: It came out of nowhere; you could step outside, turn a corner and bam! It's all over,

S: I understand now, why you always wanted me to stay sober.

F: When I saw you drunk, it was a traumatizing Déjà vu of that night, I just lost my cool,

S: Yea, I didn't mean to come over so late, acting a drunken fool.

F: Don't you know that you are the most important thing in my life?

S: (Crying) Yes, I heard the exact same words from my wife.

F: I had to bury my father because of a drink, I am not trying to bury you, my son,

S: I promise you; I promise my wife that I will not drink again. It's over, I'm done.

F: I know about your drug addiction too, we're going to help you with that as well,

S: (Crying) I'm so sorry dad, I promise I will be a better son, I promise I will get well.

F: (Crying) Come here; I love you. You're my boy, you're my son.

S: (Crying) I love you too. I didn't mean to hurt anyone.

F: You were hurting yourself the most. But I'm got you son, I got the help you need, I have the connections,

S: Thank you dad; thank you for not giving up on me and steering me in the right direction.

Can She Forgive Him (08/18/20 7:20 PM)

Father: I really don't know what to say right now, I'm at a loss for words,

Daughter: I don't even want to look at you right now. You weren't at a loss for touching me, but you're at a loss for words?

F: Every single day that I wake up, I regret it. I regret what I did to you,

D: What you did; God I wish I could just get rid of you.

F: I'm so, so sorry baby. You were just a little girl,

D: (Crying) Don't call me baby! I am not your baby; you are the sickest bastard in the whole world.

F: I know I need help; I promise you I will change,

D: The hell with your promises; just stay away from me at the farthest range.

F: I am sorry for causing you much suffering, so much pain,

D: You are a predatory monster; you were fucking insane.

F: Can you ever forget what I had done to you? Can you ever forgive me?

D: You are asking for a miracle; it's like asking a blind man if he can ever see.

F: I don't know what else to do, I don't know what else to say,

D: You're in prison now; I'll let God deal with you on Judgment day.

F: Yes, I am in prison; I pray that God forgives and has a place in heaven reserved for me,

D: I pray you go straight to hell, because that is where you deserve to be.

F: Why would you say that; wish that on your own father?

D: (Crying) Oh, so you're the victim now? From 4 to 12 you molested me; you were never my father.

F: (Crying) I know what I did was evil and wrong; I am very sorry that I hurt you, but don't hold it inside,

D: (Crying) You have no idea how much pain I've been in ever since, how many times I contemplated suicide.

F: Forgiveness; forgiving me is your only answer,

D: (Crying) None of this would have happened, if my mom didn't die from cancer.

F: I know what I did was bad, but when your mother died, I just gave up all hope,

D: Well, Karma is a bitch; and you better pray you don't drop the soap.

The Streets' Regrets (08/18/20 10:00 PM)

I am responsible for many lives taken,

Dope fiends overdosed, prostitutes murdered, families' hearts braking.

I groomed too many children; turned them into animals and goons,

Too many children stayed children, never grew up, gone too soon.

The fatal instruments of guns and bullets,

Trigger happy 12-year-olds; never afraid to pull it.

I tasted more blood than a vampire ever could; real talk,

The innocent trying to run their way home, too afraid to walk.

I never go to sleep; yet I'm so tired of people dying on me,

Garbage, rats, and cars, roadkill lying on me.

The homeless shivering in the cold, I can't keep them warm,

I can't keep them safe, can't protect them from harm.

The evil I witnessed since day one,

I'm so tired of the riots and protest, dear God, let it all be done.

"Failure is pushing yourself until you cross the finish line of success."

Save This Baby (08/18/20 11:11 PM)

Too young to get an uber, too young to be on the streets,

Bloody footprints on the streets as she walks; bare feet.

She escaped; child sex trafficking, but now she's all alone,

No place to stay, no family; no place that she can call home.

Sold by pimps, bought and kissed by predatory johns,

A filthy business; absolutely no pros, just straight cons.

Who's going to save her? She has nowhere to go,

Three o'clock in the morning, it started to snow.

Cops on the night shift; they spotted something unusual,

Bloody footprints in the snow, like a horror movie visual.

The cops followed the footprint trail and the echo of cries,

The louder the cry, the closer she was; if they don't find her, she'll die.

The cops call for her, but English is not on the tip of her tongue,

But that didn't stop her from screaming at the top of her lungs.

Cops find her in a cold, dark and snowy alley, thank God,

Cops asked her, “hablo español?” she gave them a vertical head nod.

Speaking to the cop in Spanish, the cop couldn’t control her teary eyes,

She told the cop that she’s was raped, by more than two hundred guys.

They rushed her to the hospital, her little feet were covered with blood and glass,

Cop asked the little girl why her feet were cover in blood and glass?

She told the cop how she was left in the backseat of a car,

Her pimp said, “I’ll be right back, not going too far.”

She looked around, made sure he was nowhere in sight,

She put her two bare feet together and began to kick with all her might.

She kicked and kicked; the glass was beginning to crack,

She kept looking around to make sure the pimp wasn’t coming back.

She gave one last kick to the bloody glass window,

It shattered; but only the bottom half, she had to crawl under like limbo.

THE HEALING

Pieces of glass were pierced deep into her soles,

Doctors removed them one by one; many bloody holes.

The cop who talked to her couldn't leave her side,

She told the cop in Spanish, "thank you for saving me, I really thought I would have died."

The cop said, "oh, it was fate that we found you, you're safe now baby,"

She cried to the cop, "Please, oh please, don't call me that, I'll have a panic attack if you call me baby."

The cop asked her, "Why? Why if I call you baby, you would have a panic attack?"

She said, "That is all those guys would call me, while they pinned me down, on my back."

Bless her with healing; she'll need much time,

Dear God, please let us put an end to this evil, child predatory crime.

"Anger is a bullet;

Ignorance is a knife."

"Sometimes in life, when you are a good person, you only focus on the good in other people, but you do not acknowledge the worse in people. Sometimes the worse in people outweighs the best. But that is not your fault."

The Secrets We Keep (08/19/20 11:00 PM)

Two people, one couple, last minute date,

She arrived about 30 minutes late,

Missed reservations, it's going to be a 20-minute wait.

Her; dressed in all black, as beautiful as she can be,

Exotic combination; caramel skin with blue eyes, as blue as the sea.

He had a rough day, tells her work wasn't as productive,

But he kept out how his co-worker is becoming more and more seductive.

But two can play at that game, she's not willing to lose,

He plays checkers, she plays chess; she thinks before she moves.

They finally get a table, they sit, they order,

Her phone's ringing; takes an hour to find it in her bag, she's a secret hoarder.

She looks at the screen, then looks at her man with a smirk,

Then he gets a text, it's Ms. Seduction from work.

He gets the text, she gets the call,

What kind of relationship is this? No loyalty at all.

She tells him she has to use the restroom, he said, "damn, you have to take your phone?"

She said nothing except, "I don't appreciate your tone."

He shakes his head as she walks away, sipping on his wine,

She makes her way into the restroom, facetiming her side dude; he said, "damn, you're so fine!"

She's been in there for quite some time, she's getting pretty bold,

Her man texting her saying, "you better hurry up, your food's getting cold."

What he didn't know was that she was giving her side dude an "Only fans" show,

She's really in the bathroom being a straight ho… Well, you know.

He's eating his food, text his co-worker saying, "when are you free?"

She responded, "how about right now; ditch your bitch and come see me."

He said, "Nah, I can't, I'm with my girl, we're out having dinner,"

She sent him a full nude, with the caption saying, "I guess you're not trying to be a winner."

THE HEALING

Temptation and anxiety create the ultimate sinner,

He's ready to leave his woman there, go to his co-worker, and get up in her.

She finally came out, but guess what? He ghosted her,

Left her with the bill, quickly she felt ill, but he left a note for her.

It said, "sorry babe, had to head back to the office really quick, long story. Oh, I hope you sprayed,"

She went from 0 to 100, the waiter's looking at her like, "uh, can I get paid?"

She paid the bill, so mad she stormed out, left all the food,

She opened and slammed her car door, now she's in the worst mood.

She calls her man's phone; ring, ring, he doesn't pick up,

Her anxiety is getting the best of her, having a bad case of hiccups.

She then made a call, a call to her side dude,

She said, "is it alright if I stop by? Can you put me in a good mood?"

By the look of her face, side dude is spitting raw game,

A complete mess is coming, but who will be to blame?

He arrives at his co-workers place, knocks on the door,

They kiss and hug to the bedroom, this isn't the first time, no need for a house tour.

She makes her way to her side dude, rings his bell,

Then she texts her man saying, "wait until I see you, I'm going to raise hell."

Her side dude opens his door, lets her in,

Off with her clothes, off with his; let the games begin.

One couple, two unfaithful souls, three sides to the story,

The truth is being captured on video as she says, "stop, don't record me."

Both parties are having fun on the same night,

But all it took was this one video, sent to her man; damn that side dude isn't right.

Three sides to the story; her story, his story, and the karma,

Her man was blowing up her phone, making threats saying he's going to harm her.

He said, "just wait until I see you, and I'll be waiting for your side guy,"

She responded saying, "you saw my dirt, now let me see yours, and don't lie."

Denial in his tone; he said, “I told you I had to go to the office and grab some stuff,”

She responded, “all you grabbed was her ass, and you couldn’t get enough.”

Two voices declared war; back and forth they go,

She’s calling him a dog, and he’s calling her a hoe.

Told you this would be a complete mess,

One got caught, the other won’t confess.

I’ll let you imagine the rest,

Think about it, put your mind to the test.

"It is very disturbing that there's more ways for you to become a criminal than a good human being."

Missed Kisses (08/19/20 12:14 AM)

An unwanted break up, she didn't mean what she said,

A lonely night, she couldn't sleep, alone in her bed.

Staring at her phone, hoping it lights up, hoping it rings,

Her phone lights up, dopamine released; false alarm, it's nothing.

Her tears began to water the lawn of her furry pillowcase,

Scrolling through her photos, kissing the screen as she misses his face.

She misses him so much, loved resting her head on his chest,

She misses the conversations; his pillow talks were the best.

She wants to call him, hear his voice over the phone,

She wants to say she's sorry, and that her decision is not set in stone.

No communication; it's been well over a week,

She hasn't been eating much, been feeling light-headed and weak,

Her girlfriends have been calling her, but she doesn't want to speak.

She wants him, but she's afraid he won't come back,

Paranoid; progression of depression, anxiety attacks.

What happened you may be thinking?

Well, it started on a night of heavy drinking.

They both had too much of the beery foam,

Sex was out of the question; didn't get one moan.

She goes to say, "I'm studying abroad, I'm going overseas,"

He says to her, "oh, well what about me?"

She hesitates; she doesn't know what to say,

He doesn't want her to leave, distancing herself miles away.

She then says, "I have to do what is best for me, you're simply not the best,"

Ouch, how could she say that to her lover, like shooting a cannon through his chest.

He stood there in shock, looking at her, he didn't blink,

She knew in her drunken state of mind, she spoke but didn't think.

He gathered his things and began to leave her,

She started to plead with him, but after what she said, he couldn't believe her.

She cried to him, "I didn't mean it, I didn't; it was a mistake,"

He said, “no, it is up to you on the decisions you make,”

She knew after that comment, she gave birth to his heartbreak.

She pleaded and pleaded with him some more,

Begging him not to leave, not to walk out that door.

She was grabbing him, ripped his shirt; she saw her name tatted on his chest,

She then looked up to him, and before he walked out the door, he said, “I wish you nothing but the best.”

"Money requires numbers and commas, but happiness does not. There were times I woke up in the morning, without a dime to my name. But I was happy, because I woke up that morning. There's that saying, not all money is good money. Well, I say money is not good or bad. Money is money, it is what people choose to do to get the money. People choose to do good or bad things, for the love of money."

<u>*But We Pray*</u> (08/20/20 1:14 AM)

Bills are coming, but we pray,

We make it through our darkest days.

Mental health is our true wealth,

Love does not exist if you don't love for yourself.

Heartbreak hits us, but we pray,

Wipe those tears, you will be okay.

Anyone can give you a kiss, but not everyone deserves your heart,

Just be patient, who's great for you will make their mark.

Bullies hurt the kids, but we pray,

Bullies are probably being bully at the end of the day.

Vicious cycle of child abuse,

Long absence of a father figure creates a short fuse.

Drug addictions, but we pray,

Don't leave the rehab, please stay.

So many drugs to choose from,

An overdose in the night, we lose one,

Broken relationships; fathers burying their sons.

Sex abuse, but we pray,

Her chastity was robbed from her, she wants the pain to go away.

A little girl she was, sex killed her innocence,

She's surviving; healing through her adolescence.

Racism is dividing us, but we pray,

It's killing African Americans every single day.

Human evolution, tragically reduced to black and white,

White people are treated like a beautiful day, Black people treated like a full moon thriller night.

But we pray; we pray, we pray, we pray every day,

We pray to God for deliverance, protection from the devil's way.

We pray for repentance, forgiveness and remorse,

Life is a trip; we must let it take its course.

No one is perfect; we've all told a lie,

No one is immortal, all lives eventually die.

We all have a shadow, every step of the way,

Life is a game, everyone must play,

We do not have all the rules to life, but we pray.

Make A Difference (08/21/20 1:18 PM)

High school is not his playground,

Bullies and girls tease and push him around.

He eats his lunch in the bathroom, it's his safe zone,

Eating the same peanut butter and chicken nugget sandwich since a little kid, playing games on his phone.

Upperclassmen invade his privacy, disrupts his lunch,

They knocked his sandwich out of his hands, knocked him to the ground with the hardest punch.

He finally came to; running late for class,

He looked in the bathroom mirror, bruised eye, so angry he broke the glass.

He cut his hand, cut his classes, and ran all the way home,

School was no longer part of his comfort zone.

He arrived home, parents weren't there,

He went into his bathroom with a pair of scissors, he began to cut his hair.

His curly brown locks made its way to the ground,

Thinking of all the kids picking on him, making fun of him, he just wants to leave town.

This town is no longer a place of fun,

He walks down to his basement and takes a look at his father's guns.

He knew his father's combination since he was seven,

His father even let him hold a gun when he turned eleven.

At 16, he holds that same gun in the palm of his hand,

Thinking in his mind; if you're thinking what he's thinking, he has an evil plan.

Sitting with a gun, bullets of tears,

He wants nothing but revenge on his heartless peers.

He makes his favorite sandwich, with chips and a pickle,

As he eats, he points the gun at the mirror, pretending he's Travis Bickle.

He feels empowered; nothing can hurt him, he's the man,

He's going to move forward, proceed with this horrific plan,

Dear God, place your hands on this young man if you can.

He barely slept, doesn't wake his parents, he's out the door,

If all goes tragic, his parents won't see him anymore.

Walking to his school, carrying a bag of his dad's fatal toys,

He thinks this will give him peace, closure, and eternal joy.

THE HEALING

He arrives; walking in his school's parking lot,

He saw his favorite teacher, parking in his usual spot.

His teacher didn't mention him cutting class, but admired the cutting of his hair,

That surprised him, no one ever really complimented him before, he thought no one ever cared.

His teacher said to him, "I don't care what those kids say to you, you're a winner in my book,"

That's all it took for him to change his mind, that's when he gave his teacher an eccentric look.

He told his teacher that he was coming here to get even with his peers,

His teacher said, "what do you mean get even? The bag; give it here."

His teacher opened the bag; for the love of God,

His teacher asked, "where you going to do what I think you where?" He goes up and down with an emotional head nod.

His teacher in swift shock; doesn't know what to do,

Does he tell the principal, the board, the police; he doesn't have a clue,

If you were in this teacher's position; what would you do?

"What the hell has this world come to, when we have to paint, "Black Lives Matter," in the middle of the street, just to remind the world that African American people's lives matter?"

How Many (08/21/20 6:38 PM)

How many fathers handed their sons a beer before handing them a book?

How many mothers didn't teach their daughters how to cook?

How many cops shot and killed unarmed African American women and men?

How many were acquitted, cases never opened, never spent a minute in the pen?

How many "Karens" will emerge, acting a fool?

How many parents will not send their kids back to school?

How many face masks have been used?

How many lies has Trump said, along with the words, "fake news?"

How many likes did you receive on your last post?

How many followers are real, and how many are Ghost?

How many guns are in this land?

How many countries will be banned?

How many kisses did you give your loved one on their death bed?

Who's counting right?

"When the Lord returns to this new world, people are going to want him to give them tea instead of wine."

She Kissed Him Never Again (08/21/20 7:38 PM)

He didn't cheat on her, she just had this feeling,

She doesn't want this relationship anymore, she wants healing.

He was nice to her, but he's stuck in the past,

She's up late nights thinking to herself, "this is not going to last."

He kisses her good morning, her smiles are so unreal,

Her needs and wants from him are far from being fulfilled.

She loves him, but doesn't like who he is as a person,

She wants out of this now "tolerationship" before it worsens.

She says, "I think it's best that we go our separate ways,"

He responded, "I think that is a good idea; yea, okay."

She wasn't expecting him to accept and agree,

She was expecting him to burst into tears, fall to the floor, begging on his knees.

She asked, "so, you're okay with us breaking up?"

He simply said, "Yup!"

Her curiosity was beginning to grow, so was her anger,

The conversation continued; it just got stranger and stranger.

She became desperate and asked, “so, is there someone else in the picture?”

He said, “No, but I did become fifty million dollars richer.”

She said, “what! What do you mean? How?”

He said, “My parents hit the lottery last night, they are going to cash it in right now.”

She said, “and you didn’t tell me, how did you stay so calm?”

He said, “I told you to read the bible, I told you to read Psalms.”

Fifty million dollars, and he’s their only son,

What’s theirs is his; boy he’s about to have some fun.

In her mind she’s thinking, “Oh shit,”

In his mind he’s thinking, “New chick.”

How can she bounce back? What could she say?

No kids involved, now she’ll need another place to stay.

Guess who’s on their knees, crying and begging for forgiveness,

Tables turn, her bridge is burned, no more good morning kisses.

She’ll never kiss him again, karma is that bitch,

He’s about to find him a Dorothy; guess who’s the witch?

Reunited with Her Mother (08/21/20 9:00 PM)

Unsolicited adoption; her mother kissed her and said goodbye,

No pictures, she can't remember her mother with her two-year old eyes,

But she remembers her mother's smell, her voice, she couldn't hold back her cries.

Life goes on, a young woman she has grown to be,

She's in search for her mother, applied for records; she waits, she sees.

Twenty years is a long time, a miracle is what she prays for,

A month and a half later, she's calling and asking, "what's all the delays for?"

They're searching and searching; no bad or good news,

No other information, no other clues.

Frustration in her conscious; wasn't sure if she'll ever find her,

But every day, God sent her more hope through prayer, simply to remind her.

To remind her that when there's a will, there's a way,

She found her will, on her lucky day.

She likes to drive, does a little Uber on the side,

A customer shows up on her map; she accepts, but it's going to be a long ride.

The customer comes out; middle-aged guy with a bag,

They introduced each other; corky guy with no swag.

They started a conversation, he said, "I'm going to meet my wife at the airport,

She was rushing so fast; she completely forgot her passport."

She said, "aww, that's too bad, is she going to miss her flight?"

He said, "No, her flight is not until later tonight."

She said, "Wow, what a nice husband you are to go all this way to bring it to her,"

He responded, "yea, that's my wife Hali, God I love her."

She swerved on the road the moment she heard the name Hali,

Her heart skipped a beat, an actual miracle in reality.

She apologized saying, "I'm so sorry sir! Thought I saw a raccoon,

But not to worry, we will arrive at the airport soon."

He said, "oh, that's okay, I've experienced far worse Uber drivers,"

She's feeling like she's found treasure, deep in the ocean as a scuba diver.

This Uber ride is a trip, but life is a game,

What are the odds; Hali is her biological mother's name.

She asked the customer, "if you don't mind, what is your wife's maiden name?

He said, "it is Salley; I know, Hali Salley-Steinberg, what a name."

A watery vision; her eyes began to tear up as she drives,

That is her mother's name; Hali Salley, her prayers have arrived.

She asked him, "Do you have a picture of your wife?"

He responded, "Oh sure," and pulled out his phone; he swipes and swipes.

He says, "Here's my beautiful wife, and our baby girl Tiffany,"

She couldn't hold it in anymore, and asked him, "do you have any tissues for me?"

He asked, "oh my God, are you okay?"

She responded, "I'm sorry, but you just made my day."

Confusion in the car, he asked her, "what do you mean?"

She said, "I was adopted, my biological mother's name is Hali Salley, it's like a dream."

In shock, he said to her, "you have got to be kidding me?"

He said it again, "you have got to be kidding me!"

She responded saying, "No, I kid you not mister,

This is my first time seeing her since I was two, and I have a kid sister?"

He says, "oh my sweet Lord, Are you Star?"

She said, "yes," as she's trying to keep herself together in the car.

Tears begin to fall down his face, he calls his wife,

He's about to give her the greatest news of her life.

He calls and says, "Hali, I'm on my way, and there is someone I want you and Tiffany to meet,"

Hali says, "Oh, well okay then. Oh, by the way, they bump us up to first class seats; isn't that sweet?"

He said, "yea, but in a few minutes, you might want to take a different seat."

They arrived at the airport, he asked Star, "Are you ready?"

Star says, "I feel like I'm on cloud 9, trying to keep myself steady."

THE HEALING

He holds her hand and said, “you’ll be fine,”

They go in, there she is, her mother and sister waiting in line,

Star at twenty-two years old now; seeing her mother, only for the second time.

He holds her hand, they walk forward to them,

Hali sees her husband, gives a strange look, thinking, “who’s that young woman with him?”

The closer they get, the clearer she sees who Star is,

Hali looking at Star, all Hali could say was, “well, there she is.”

I guess a mother could never forget her daughter,

Both their faces were covered with teary water.

They both broke down and hugged each other so tight,

They just squeezed each other, with all their might.

Hali couldn’t get over how much they looked the same,

Star understood why she couldn’t find her; she went by her married name.

Star said to her mother, “I dreamt of finding you my whole life, I can’t believe it’s you,”

Hali said, “baby, this feels like a dream, it doesn’t feel true,”

Hali introduced Star to her little sister, Tiffany said in her sweet voice, “it’s nice to meet you.”

So much to catch up on, it’ll take more than this night,

They’re not getting on that plane now, cancelled flight.

She’s found her; I told you today was her lucky day,

I also said that when there’s a will, there’s a way.

A daughter, reunited with her mother, God is in his heaven,

Star and her mother Hali took a selfie, shared it on social media, and posted their story at 11:11.

The Lost Daughter (01/31/11)

She wakes up;
As she walks out to her balcony,
To bear witness of this beautiful morning.
She feels reborn,
She feels miraculously safe.
She lives one day at a time
From an unbearable tragic life.
A life no human being should have ever lived,
Not even an animal.
Once upon her time;
She had a mother, a father.
They loved her more than
Anyone could ever be loved.
They loved her excessively.
One late night;
Her mother and father argued.
Her at eight years old,
Hears her mother scream "Divorce,"
A word she does not understand.
Not much later; big bang!
A bang that changes her universe,
Her life, forever.
The daughter hears hysterical screams,
She runs to her two parents,
To find only one still breathing.
The daughter sees "suicide,"
Another word that this 8-year-old does not understand.
Her mother takes her out of the disturbing sight,
She calls for her father to wake up;
Wake up from his 357. Magnum coma,

But he is gone.
The daughter cries tears of confusion as
Her mother cries tears of sudden guilt.
Time goes by; 3 years.
Mother weds again.
Through the mother's eyes;
A husband, a lover.
Through daughter's eyes;
A monster with an evil mission.
One night her mother is not home.
The daughter on the couch,
Sitting beside her, her nightmare.
Out of nowhere, he begins to say things to her.
Things that an 11-year-old should never hear,
Things he would only say to her mother.
His words transformed into touches,
Sick, perverted touches.
At her innocent young age;
She does not get an epiphany of
What is going on, but she's not comfortable.
As she tries to leave,
His touches transformed into grabs,
She screams and screams,
Yet no one hears her,
As if she is a ghost.
He drags her into her room,
Slams and locks the door,
With him inside there with her.
No words ever created,
Can explain what evil went on in that room,
Or what he did to her.
Morning comes, she sees her mother.

THE HEALING

The daughter does not mention a word,
Not even a letter of what happened to her.
More time goes by:
Her mother begins to wonder
Why her daughter retires for the night
On the couch rather than her bed.
So many tears were cried,
So many frightening nightmares,
So many more of his demonic caresses,
His derange ambition for rape.
She cannot take it anymore.
She cannot stay in her room,
She cannot tell her mother,
She cannot tell anyone; she is lost.
Another late night;
She hears her mother arguing
With her devilish husband,
A Deja vu of the night four years ago.
Her mother screams "divorce" again,
A word the daughter still does not understand,
But is expecting to hear the big bang.
She hears the big bang,
She hears it 4 times.
The daughter is shocked at first.
But she is relieved, thinking her nightmare is gone.
She begins to realize that this night
is different from the other.
She does not hear her mother scream,
Yet she hears laughter.
She runs to the room,
Expecting to see her mother standing tall,
Her mother is lying dead

With the four big bangs pierced in her body.
She sees "murder," another word she does not understand.
Her nightmare stands there
With his drunken voice, saying humorously;
"Four wasted years equals four bullets."
She thought her nightmare was over,
He just got stronger.
She sees her mother being thrown
Away as if she is garbage.
He takes her away,
She begins a devastating journey into
A very hell bound, dark world.
God help her, please help her.
She lived with her nightmare for
Many more unimaginable years.
He turned her into a sex slave,
Into a drug-addicted prostitute,
Locked up in his basement prison,
Those abusive nights and horrific years.
Yet from all those years,
She gained some knowledge.
She now understands the meaning of "divorce,"
The definition of suicide,
The definition of murder.
She had to escape her nightmare,
This lost daughter had to find her way out.
She had to make a decision,
She had a question like Hamlet.
Either she lives by committing murder,
Killing her nightmare of a stepfather.
Or she dies by committing suicide.
She made her decision.

THE HEALING

He comes to her for his
Night of pleasure, with a pair of scissors,
With a vision of her with shorter hair.
She sees the scissors; she sees her moment.
She sees her chance to escape her nightmare.
As he goes to chip away at her hair,
She uses the knowledge she gained as
A sex slave, seducing-him, making him
Feel more comfortable.
Her plot worked beautifully.
She grabbed the scissors,
And with all her might,
Plus, the strength of God,
She stabbed away.
Now she is standing tall.
All she had to say to him
During the last beats of his
Satanic black heart was;
"Seven years of horrific torture,
Seven years of this horrible nightmare,
Equals seven stabs, plus the power of Karma."
No one could probably imagine
How this young girl survived.
Living through seven years of molestation,
Seven years of abuse; of rape.
Suffering the instant loss of her
Father, of her mother,
Being kidnapped, being lost.
Her troubled time is past her now.
Now at her adult age;
She is healing, slowly but surely.
She is filtering all the poisons from her body.

Yet she still feels somewhat lost.
She lost the love she once had from her parents.
People would wonder what will happen to this girl.
Is she going to be alright,
Will she live on and be happy?
What is next for this lost daughter?
Tomorrow, I guess.

"I would like to dedicate this poem to all of the women, the young girls, all of the lost daughters around the world. The women who have endured such heinous, traumatic, and unforgettable pain; of verbal, physical, and sexual abuse. There are much better days waiting for you." -Jordan Wells

The Contract of Goodbye (08/22/20 10:34 PM)

She loved him and he loved her,

They were once happy together, until trouble occurred.

Their bond has been invaded,

Their love connection has unfortunately faded.

Smells like a divorce, bring on the lawyers, papers, and pens,

A love that was so strong, but can't survive, can't win.

She's had enough, he's had too much,

Ten years together; over and over, the same old touch.

They grew apart, it happens to the best of us,

The ping pong of lies, a loss of trust.

Both their eyes set on another,

His eyes are now for her girlfriend, and hers are on his brother, from another mother.

He has a business; my is it doing so well,

She has the divorce papers, to him, they are the papers from hell.

He reads the papers; page by page,

He can't read or see straight; filled with anger and rage.

Attorneys are the coach, but the two are the players,

She wants half of everything, possessions are in layers.

Too much money for him to split it 50/50,

He's going to lose his mind; he'll go 51/50.

She wants that half, no more, no less,

He's in for a long one, with two kids, here comes the child support stress.

I could go on and on; if you're married, no worries, this doesn't refer to you,

I seriously doubt that either one of them will say, "I'm going to miss you."

Enslaved Materialized (08/22/20 11:06 PM)

Cash in the vault, let's go get a Benz,
Diamonds are a woman's best friend, watch how much you spend.
Can't just buy regular sneakers, got to be Jordan's or Yeezy,
No more quarters for the pay toll, everyone passes with EZ.
Too many clothes, not enough parties or events,
Now they sell the clothes, have to pay the rent.
Jet plane selfies; look ma, I'm wealthy,
Mentally unhealthy; ma, help me, help me!
Brand New products on the shelves,
Christmas time; here comes Santa and his elves.
The green paper is the army, the plastic cards are taking over the land,
Cryptocurrency; no more cash, no more bank robberies, hackers and pirates are about to expand.
Still buying materials, boost the economy,
Debt makes me sick, it put the con in me.
Do you like being enslaved to a product or service?
First of the month, short on rent, doesn't that make you nervous?
Thousand-dollar concert ticket, for a 3-hour show?
Phones out recording the whole time, thousands of these gadgets flickers and glows.

Ads on social media, be careful what you search,
Before there was super chat, there were collection plates in a church.
Handouts, donations and gifts,
Stock market crashing as if it drove off a cliff.
The more commas they see,
The more corrupt they be.
5k bags, "living my best life" hashtag,
Fronting and stunting, but don't mean to brag,
All that materialism can't create swag.
Flat screen TVs, flat screen phones,
Where's the plastic CDs, different sound with digital tones.
Waiting in long lines, it's stretches around the block,
Waiting for the same phones, with the same screens, the same clock.
Treating investments like the last kid to be picked,
Broke like a joke, more like a cheesy magician performing the last trick.
It's Covid-19's world now, business is put on hold,
Things aren't being bought, things aren't being sold,
COVID has a second coming, as soon as it gets cold.
How bad do you want that new car, new truck?
Oh, you have something to sell, but not buy? Well, good luck.

Animals (08/23/20 11:11 PM)

Birds free in the sky,

Birds in the grease, deep fry.

Cows on a farm go moo,

Cows in a pot, beef stew.

Pigs oink and squeal,

Pigs' throats slit; they're killed.

Chickens, turkeys, ducks; they have a taste,

Tons of their flesh recalled; such a waste.

Heart disease, high blood pressure, heart attacks and strokes,

Meat is the reason why many people start to choke.

Health issues on the rise,

People saying, "protein comes from animals," that's a lie.

It comes from the feed of grass and grains,

Feeding ourselves dead flesh, slowly deteriorates our brains.

It's hard to let go of something that has been your whole life,

You may want to think twice before carving turkeys with a knife.

Millions have to die because their smell and taste are great,

Remove them from your diet, before it's too late.

We can't keep putting the blind eye, what about the environment?

It is time you take a carnivore retirement.

Is plant base the way to go? Your choice not mine,

Food for thought, you may choose not, and that is swine,

Oops, I mean that is fine.

Innovative Beauty (08/24/20 4:10 PM)

The rise of the sun,

The birth of a daughter or son.

The blossom of a flower,

The completion of the Freedom Tower.

The sound of an infant's first word,

The sound of chirpings from a baby bird.

The new idea becomes a new way of living,

The new wealth creates a new way of giving.

"You're too alive to linger in the past, trying to reincarnate something that was never even born."

A Father's Love (08/24/20 11:46 PM)

His seed is born, premature plan,
He's a father now, but not quite a man.
Stuck between 18 and 19, with a brand-new kid,
Instagram stories of his son, 15-second vids.
Young mother sleeps as father holds his son,
Serious responsibility; he can't hide, he can't run.
But he doesn't want to run, he sees his son, he sees himself,
The greatest gift from God is a child; a father's wealth.
Late night cries coming from the crib,
Onesies, diapers, feeding; where's the bib?
He sees his son crawl, walks, daddy is his first word,
He picks his son up, toss him in the air, flying like a bird,
He hears his sons laughter, the most beautiful sound he's ever heard.
He's hard at work, a picture of his son on his desk,
Family man and college man, studying for a test,
Young couple having issues, separation is what's best.
Lord have mercy, she's taking him to court,
Lies pouring out of her, saying, "your honor, he didn't even want this child, he was begging me to abort."
The lies fueled his anger, judge says, "you're not mentally stabled to rise this innocent child,

You stand clear of them, restraining order; keep your distance at least a quarter mile."
She takes his money, and takes his son,
The stress in his brain, flowing through his veins, he's at his temple with his gun.
A situation from hell, his son is growing older,
Baby mama drama, her horns are showing, she's becoming colder.
A father's love is being blocked,
She treats their son like he's a share of stock,
Son is now a pre-teen, can't stop the clock.
Father's missed a lot of time, she should be ashamed,
Every so often, he sees his son playing his basketball games.
He reaches over to greet his son, but his son sees him as a stranger,
The father doesn't know if he should be heartbroken or show anger.
A mother's brainwashed strategy works to perfection,
He sees so much of himself in his son, it's like the perfect reflection.
A young son is a young man now, child support reached the finished line,
But now the son doesn't want no relationship, thinks it's a waste of time.
Until one day, the son felt ill, like never before,

THE HEALING

Nausea, headaches, and feeling sore.
The father gets a call, "your son is in the hospital,"
Father says, "what! What happened? I just saw him at the game, how's this possible?"
Doctors run test, bad news in his blood,
Leukemia has invaded him, turning his blood into mud.
The father's only son is fighting for his life now,
All this time, he's asking God, "why my son, why now?"
The father prays to God, prays for his son's life to be spared,
Father's at the hospital, baby mother looks as if she doesn't care.
She walks out; now a father and son moment in time,
Son asked, "what are you doing here? You can leave, I'll be just fine."
The father responded, "regardless of what your mother has said, I never stopped loving you my son,
I was there when you were born, changed your diapers, feeding you, we had so much fun."
He said to his son, "I had some blood drawn, no need to fish, I'm the catch,
I will be your bone marrow donor, it's the perfect match."
His crying son saying, "You mean I'm not going to die?"
The father said, "not on my watch, I got you my son; please don't cry."
A father and son, reunited under difficult circumstances,

But you just never know when God will bless you with those second chances.

Throw away the grudges, why bother?

You're too alive, love thy father.

Can't Help Who You Love (08/25/20 4:44 PM)

They broke up a long time ago, but the love never died,
Separated physically while the love kept growing inside.
She thought of him, he thought of her,
Parallel destinies, miracles occur.
The universe had a plan to reunite the two,
It is always meant to be when the love is always true.
A party is to come, both invited, but coming with different groups,
A dance party; switching partners, it comes full circle like a loop.
They come to each other, face to face, a surprising glance,
Hundreds of feet on the floor, but their four feet decided not to dance.
Separated for years, here they are, at the same time and place,
A hug that squeezed out forgiveness, she tippy-toes a kiss to his handsome face.
Back and forth they go as they start the reminiscing,
The arguments of jealousy, hurt, suspicions, and what was missing.
She told him she loved him, but when she left, he didn't chase,
He told her that he feared he wasn't the only one in the race,
He said he feared not winning first place.

A conversation on a midnight balcony; drifting away into the moonlight,
They took their words and had a dance, not a verbal fight.
They acknowledged their mistakes,
They regret their heated debates,
This moment is a scene out of a movie, and this is their second take.
They kindled their love again, lit up the night sky, oh how jealous is the moon?
Love is the pleasure of life they feast; he's the fork, she's the spoon.
Let the knife cut out the toxins, doubts, and the poisonous past,
May this immortal love resurrect a bond that will forever, eternally last.

Pride in Her Body (08/25/20 9:44 PM)

She's not your ideal model of thin and tall,
She's thick and voluptuous, and she's not ashamed at all.
Curvy with a small waist and wide hips,
A belly that sticks out, a belly she can grip.
A top-heavy bust,
Double-D bras are a must,
She walks with pride through the men who drools with lust.
With lips like Angelina Jolie, she could make millions with a kissing booth,
The numbers on a scale are not her enemy, but simply her truth.
Her truth is not what she hides, nor does it discourage her,
She wears what makes her feel good, her self-esteem encourages her.
Negative comments on the gram,
Blocks them like they're spam,
Here's another selfie for her haters; BAM!
Been a little chubby her whole life,
Not once has she thought of going under the knife,
She's comfortable in her own skin, she'll make an incredible wife.
Never mind her weight;
Don't make her wait.

Don't worry about her size,

When you speak to her, look her in those beautiful eyes.

The larger her body, the larger a man's respect should be,

Beauty is skin deep, not the barbie doll imagery programmed by society.

Her thickness is her richness,

Her curves are what she deserves,

Her body is oh so Godly,

Let her live, let her live.

Numerical Riddles (08/25/20 10:36 PM)

You can see me on a couple of goats,
When they jump high, they float.
What am I?
I am every winner's dream,
An artist only wants me when their album streams.
What am I?
You need me if you want to drink,
If you're beneath me, man you stink.
What am I?
I rhyme with the name Kevin,
I'm close with my midnight brethren.
What am I?
If you divide me by 3, you'll get five,
If you multiply me by one, I shall arrive.
What am I?
If you put me before candles, I make a beautiful song,
If you put me after sweet, I can't go wrong.
What am I?

(*Marry the ABC's and 123's to understand.*
You figure out what they are and sleep on it,
By morning, you'll already know the answer.)

"These platforms want you to do something controversial, then they remove your content because it goes against the grain, and then you become a victim, and you begin to post your victimization, and that is what makes you famous. Being a victim is the new superhero."

Queen Virgin (08/26/20 2:14 PM)

Untouched; all the way to the age of thirty-three,

A few innocent kisses but haven't dismissed her virginity.

Her naked anatomy has only been for baths and showers,

She owns her chastity; she has the power.

She's had her interest, but still she reserves it,

She hasn't met the right one, the one who she feels deserves it.

A lonely night in a crowded club,

Steam and mist floating up above.

Through the mist and hundreds of dancing feet,

There comes a goddess, an unexpected meet and greet.

A new friend, she shakes her hand while her other hand holds a drink,

Her friend tells her she'll be right back, gives her a seductive wink,

She's back in a flash, didn't have a chance to blink.

Her friend is tall like a model, right out of a dream,

Cocoa butter scented skin under a tank top and skinny fitted jeans,

Her friend whispered in her ear and asked, "Can I lick you like ice cream?"

That whisper in her ear triggered something in her brain,

Like a vocal key unlocking the doors of her sexuality, she thinks she's insane,
But she didn't resist, she didn't complain.
Her friend takes her by her hand, pulls her like a current into an ocean of dancing,
A companionship founder; sinking in romancing.
Then there's the first kiss, a kiss while they dance,
A kiss she never had, a kiss of chance.
They made their way into the men's restroom; oops, drunken gals,
Yet they received no disturbance, dirty talking to each other's ear canals.
Smeared makeup faces, grazing of tongues,
Not giving themselves time to breathe, they separate to welcome more air in their lungs.
Back to kissing; kissing in the Uber, all the way home,
They make it to her home, ripped off their clothes, a duet of moans.
Two sexy women on the couch, then the shower, a sacred affection,
Finally landed on the bed, a wet and naked reflection,
Her foggy thoughts of her sexuality have become a clearer perception.
She lays on her back; this virgin queen will be giving and receiving a vaginal knighting,

THE HEALING

Nipple and lip biting,
Hair pulling and moan reciting,
Her friend is in control, she's doing the guiding.
Queen Virgin; back arched while she moans to the ceiling,
Oh, she's never felt this before, my God what a feeling,
A lonely soul, a tongue counter-clocking her pink hole, she's found her healing.
Heavy breathing; misty romance dancing in the air,
Her friend laying on top of her, playing with her damped hair.
Gazing at each other with satisfied eyes,
A true orgasm she felt, one she could never deny.
A kiss to her clammy frontal lobe, her friend said, "that was so much fun,"
They closed their eyes, wrapped together like a human bun,
Destined for parallel dreams, almost time for the rising sun.
The morning has arrived, she's gained her full serenity,
A new woman who's found herself, she's found her identity,
This queen now bids farewell to her 33-year old virginity.

"Fame is just a wall that people will eventually tear down to get to you. Don't be the wall."

Stay True to You (08/26/20)

Release the pain from within,
Forgive yourself for all your sins.
Let go of the hurt you felt from the past,
Dismiss it from your heart, don't make it last.
People are people, stuck in misery and can't get out,
People getting involved with other people's business, have no idea what they're talking about.
Stay true to yourself, it doesn't cost to be free,
Mental health is mental wealth, take your time and always believe.

"There's only one thing that will set African Americans free, and that is OWNERSHIP."

Goodbye His Friend (08/27/20 6:16 PM)

He was like his brother,
A dear friend like no other,
A tragic morning, a tragic call from his friend's mother.
Her screams and cries,
Bad news to his ears, his best friend has died,
He took a sad direction; he chose the suicide.
Yesterday he said hello to his friend, but didn't get to say goodbye,
He wants to text his friend and ask him, "why?"
Been best friends since they were five,
Hurt that his friend is gone, and he's still alive.
He's angry, painful thoughts of why he chose to leave,
He doesn't want this on his conscious, he doesn't want to grieve.
Laying in his room; tear, after tear, after tear,
He would give anything to go to his friend's house, knock on the door, and his friend just appears.
A friendship lost, no answers for closure,
No signs, no warnings, his friend showed no exposure.
His partner in crime, used to chase the same girls,
Then they chased dreams, set out to conquer the world.
He couldn't post a memorial picture, too painful for likes and views,

He doesn't want to be the one to share such horrifying news.
He goes to see his friend's mother, one brief kiss on her cheek,
One long hug; many tears they share together, they are emotionally weak.
He asked her if she had any ideas of why,
She said, "I knew he was depressed, but he wouldn't talk to me, no matter how much I tried."
He takes her hand, and prays with his friend's mother;
"*Dear Lord; we ask that you watch over my friend, my brother,*
I ask that you watch over his sisters and his mother.
I ask that you forgive and allow him through the gates,
I ask that you give us some healing for why he couldn't wait.
I ask that you give us the strength to make it through this difficult time,
I ask that you watch and protect my best partner in crime.
(Crying) Lastly father, I want to say thank you for bringing him into not just their lives, but my life,
He was the greatest friend anyone could ever have in this life.
Until we meet again, let us say amen,
As I say goodbye, goodbye my friend.

God & Satan (1/17/14)

God: The time has come for us to talk; Jesus is coming forward to once again make his mark,

Satan: You disease us with Jesus, your time is too late, the earth will flood with eternal dark.

God: Your plan will fail, putting an end to your wicked spell;

Satan: My plans are in order, can't you tell, welcome to my kingdom of pure hell.

God: Those souls are mines to keep, not yours;

Satan: Then, why such curiosity of me? Always knocking on my doors.

God: You feed them poison, so swiftly to tell a lie;

Satan: They sell me their souls, so promptly, I shall buy.

God: I will end your demonic contracts, stop your evil deals

Satan: Stop me if you dare, if you will; the news is on, I see more kills.

God: You think you have control because you influenced to make a gun?

Satan: I know I have control because my way is so much fun.

God: This universe I will heal; this world I will fix,

Satan: My worshipping patients will only come to their
Dr. Six, Six, Six.

God: You think you're so unique, so divine, so funny.

Satan: I think I have more believers than you, by the love and power of money.

God: You're responsible for wars, drugs, AIDS; what's next?

Satan: Hmmm. World War 3, legalize coke and weed, metastasize unprotected sex.

God: You were an angel, why did you choose to fall?

Satan: You knew I was too greedy; it was a must that I have it all.

God: Look at what you did; yet there's more evil you want to achieve?

Satan: No, I made an offer they couldn't refuse; they ask, they shall receive.

God: What will you do? What other sadistic plans are you going to sell?

Satan: Sorry, confidential plans; my leaders under oath will soon show, never tell.

God: Just like the plan of those hijacked planes?

Satan: Yes! Oh, how I pleasure evil thoughts dancing in their brains.

God: You dare show your flaming face in the towers on that September 11th day?

Satan: I was happy as HELL; I wanted to come out and play.

God: You may be strong; but I am much mightier, much stronger;

Satan: You may be loved, but fear is what lasts longer.

God: You've poisoned their minds, souls, and bodies; getting them to kill and eat the flesh of my animals;

Satan: Oh, my Lucifer, wait until they kill them all; your human race will become human cannibals.

God: Some battles of Good and evil you may have won; you will never win this WAR;

Satan: Are you sure? We shall see what the future has in store.

"People grow up so misinformed. They become so concerned about having their own car, having their own place, but they never focus on having their own business. Their own company."

God & Satan Pt. 2 (08/27/20 9:48 PM)

God: It's been six years since we've last talked, look at what you've done,

Satan: Ah six, my favorite number; give me three and let's have some fun.

God: People are dying all over the earth by your wicked virus; I warn you, this better stop,

Satan: I can't help it; I need more demons, more scheming, more satanic cops.

God: Eight minutes and forty-six seconds; you're grooming psychopathic cowards,

Satan: 8:46; remember that number? It's when the plane hit the first tower.

God: Yes, you showed your horns that day, I'll never forgive you for that,

Satan: I'm not asking for forgiveness; I don't even ask for you to take me back.

God: 2020 was supposed to be a special year, you made it a living hell,

Satan: There you go, blaming me for everything gone wrong, I told you six years ago; my leaders under oath will soon show but never tell.

God: Back to these cops, their duty is to protect and serve,

Satan: Their minds belong to me; their new duty is to pile up dead protesters and start a purge.

God: You're dead wrong; but I have something for your ass,

Satan: What? Another preacher who begs for donations, just so they can fly in first class?

God: No, my one begotten son will one day make his return,

Satan: Ah, him again huh? That is the very least of my concerns.

God: I told you that you will never win this war,

Satan: Well, let me tell you something that I never shared before.

God: What exactly is that?

Satan: As long as I have music, I can't lose it.

As long as I have their souls, they will always pay the toll.

As long as there's bullets and guns, may they forever pull it, have some bloody fun, because there's nowhere to run.

As long as there's "Black Lives Matter," the greed of corporate America will grow fatter and fatter.

As long as black people are identified as black, they will keep getting shot in the back.

God: Black and white was your recipe for disaster,

Satan: We had nations to build, slavery just built them faster.

God: I hope Hitler and the others are equally burning in hell,

Satan: Oh, that is my man; I hate to brag, but you know I thought him well.

God: You've caused so much evil these past six years,

Satan: I know; I love it, I cherish it, I love seeing the innocent crying guilty tears.

God: This is not a game; if necessary, I will hit the reset button,

Satan: You're insane; you do that and there will be nothing.

God: You betrayed the deal of balance; now there's no deal,

Satan: I did not betray it; I just wrote in the fine print, "shoot to kill."

God: You have gone beyond too far; you've caused everlasting, unapologetic scars,

Satan: You made me; you sent me down there remember? I can only go deep, never far.

God: Yes, I sent you down there; you tried to portray me and got out of hand,

Satan: I wanted everything; the praises and prayers, you of all should understand.

God: I gave you music and songs, but you influenced the angels to do wrong,

Satan: I can't help it if I have fans; they always come to my door and hit the bell, ding-dong.

God: To my children; give your life to me, I will show you the way,

Satan: To my Satanist; I'll give you more money than you can ever dream; in return, I'll need your soul okay?

God: No, do not give him a thing, don't listen to what he has to say,

Satan: Follow me, I'll give you all the gold, diamonds, and cars; eternal pay.

God: He will give you nothing but hell and demons in your brain,

Satan: I can give you everything you've always wanted, all you have to do is say, "HAIL" along with my name.

God: My children, stay away from him; he's nothing but trouble, and bloodshed pain,

Satan: He's just mad because I'm ahead in this political game.

God: Truth be told your soul is worth more than silver and gold,

Satan: No, without money, your ass will be homeless, praying for warmth in the freezing cold.

God: Ignore his lies and always pray,

Satan: But when you die, what will he have to say?

God: My children, don't lose your faith, don't lose hope,

Satan: Oh of course, don't lose hope; just let your sons be an altar boy, and pray he doesn't drop the soap.

God: My children; I will forgive you for your sins, but if you bow to this dark angel, you will never win,

Satan: Silence! I'm watching The Exorcist; I just love it when her head spins.

God: Always come to me children; come for forgiveness and healing,

Satan: My leaders are already working on the next virus and disease; Lucifer, we are going to make a 2030 killing,

But sorry, we love our secrets; this will be the special "tea" worth not spilling.

"You know, there was a time when people could just say whatever was on their mind, and people would just ignore them and their opinions. Whatever happened to that? People don't ignore anymore, they always respond."

Heels, Dollars, and Life (Unknown Date)

Her eyes on the mirror, looking at her face;

She's on a paper chase, more like a paper race.

Putting on her makeup; fixing up her hair;

She steps outside the dressing room, but her mind says, "don't you dare!"

She goes out; surrounded by wolves, pigs, and trolls,

She feels like Jesus being crucified; instead of the cross, she's hanging from poles.

All eyes on her, like a professor in a class;

What's going through her mind; while they're grabbing and smacking her ass.

Familiar dollars coming from stranger's hands,

The whispers of doom in her ears; offers requested for one-night stands.

Pulling her by her wrist, "let me get a dance;"

Not her cup of tea, but her job requires she takes that chance.

Dead presidential grass blankets the dance floor,

Dancing in those high heels all night, her feet are swollen and sore.

More and more liquor, Hennessy running through her bloodstreams;

A private dance; living her nightmares, while he's living his dreams.

Many nights intoxicated; her body's num, can't feel a thing;

All night long, her ass is smacked, it no longer stings.

End of the night, the heels are off; she's counting that money;

She wants out but needs in, bills and babies are no joke; no freebies honey.

A lot on her mind, but her family don't want to hear what she has to say;

Judging her like there's no tomorrow, she's only human at the end of the day.

She cried many tears, but always wiped them away;

The hell what her family thinks or what anyone has to say.

Looking in the mirror again, just asking herself, "how?"

Tupac said, "*protect your essence, you are still precious, smile for me now.*"

Venting and Healing (08/29/20 11:18 AM)

So, I figured we can take a brief little intermission. Not to worry, the journey is not quite over yet. We still have a bit more to go. However, there is something I would like to share with you. Even thou this is not a poem, this is a message I would like for you, the reader, to think about. There are some very tragic and traumatizing events that are happening in today's world. Where do I begin?

I mean with this whole Covid-19 pandemic, to the consistent police shootings of unarmed African American men and women. To the politics of American society, people in debt, unemployed, facing eviction, and the problems grow without solutions. I really want to talk about these acts of evil; these police shootings. Let me start with the fatal shooting of a twenty-six-year-old African American woman named Breonna Taylor, who was gunned down in her own home, by police. When I heard about this, and begin to look into this more, I said to myself, "When are they going to learn?"

That is the burning question I have; when will they learn? Who are *they* you be asking? The law enforcement departments, the law makers, the actual police officers who seem to have trigger happy fingers, and who uses piss poor judgment on how they execute investigations. I understand that people are only human. However, these fatal mistakes are becoming the norm, as well as there being no consequences for these particular officers who are literally getting away with murder.

No accountability whatsoever, no remorse, no compassion, absolutely no empathy for their actions. I am by no way saying that every single police officer is committing these acts of hate. Obviously that is not an accurate analysis. But there are certain individuals who are defending these actions and the horrifying behavior of these law enforcement officers. Which brings me to another tragedy, the murder, the public lynching of another African American, George Floyd. Eight minutes and forty-six seconds. That is the amount of time that demonic terrorist placed his knee on George Floyd's neck, until he killed him. I am not even going to write his name in my book; not him or his other three helpers. To this day, I cannot watch the whole video. It is way too painful, infuriating, and inhumane. What was going on in his mind? That police officer I am referring to? What kind of thoughts were going on in his brain, for him to literally kneel on a man's neck, for a whole eight minutes and forty-six seconds?

Only a demon can be capable to commit that act of evil. Remember what I said earlier? About the whole black and white definitions? I know many of you may completely disagree with me on my opinions about black and white but allow me to speak on that again when it comes to the George Floyd situation. Again, the definitions of "black" are, "*hostile; threatening; without any moral quality or goodness; evil; wicked; gloomy, and harmful.*"

Now as I said earlier, those definitions do not define me as a man, or as a human being. I am a proud African American man. I am a proud man of African descent. That is how I define myself. But now let me give you the definitions of white again; the definitions of "white" are, "*Morally pure; innocent; fortunate, harmless, and without malice.*"

Now that I gave you those definitions again, ask yourself, in that video, did you see any *purity*, any *innocence*, with what that "white" police officer did to George Floyd? Was that "white" police officer behaving "*without malice*" or being "*harmless*?" NO! absolutely not. There was nothing pure, innocent, or harmless about that man, or what he did to George Floyd. But I will tell you what that "white" police officer was in that moment. He was evil, wicked, hostile, threatening, without moral quality or goodness; he was harmful, and he came with all the malice.

So, technically speaking, he's the "black" guy, by definition. Think about that; take a few minutes as you are reading this, and truly think about it. Do we as African American people, truly want to continue to identify ourselves as "black" people? Do we want to continue to accept this definition of who we are, or who we are supposed to be, as a people? African American people have been looked upon as evil, wicked, and violent people for so long, since the very beginning. You see that on television, the characters we portray are thugs, gangsters, criminals, "black" guys. The term "black" is a tainted definition of who we are. "White" people have been programmed to see us as such, to the point where it does not matter how successful we are in this country, in this world, we are still looked upon as the bottom of the barrel. We are still looked upon as "black" thugs, convicts, troubled, violent individuals.

I honestly believe that is why so many "black on black" incidents occur on a daily basis. We have been programmed to see ourselves as thugs and criminals. That is why so many young African American individuals feel the pressure to join the gangs in their environments, the peer pressure to indulge in drugs and alcohol. Because in general, we do not see value in ourselves, we were not taught to see ourselves as human beings. That is why is it just as easy for us to kill ourselves, as it is for a non-African American person to kill us.

We have been deliberately trained to hate ourselves, to see ourselves as "niggas" who will never amount to anything or will never be missed. Even if we do make it out, through athletics or entertainment, we still have a bitter relationship. I am beginning to believe now that it is not entirely about jealousy, why there are so many "black on black" incidents. I believe it is simply because we were brainwashed to hate ourselves. We have been programmed to view ourselves as these wicked, evil people who cannot be trusted, and some of us have been so programmed, that some live up to the expectations of being a violent, evil, wicked person. We have to eliminate in our consciousness, these false definitions of who we are in this society. We have to begin the process of seeing ourselves as African Americans, as human beings; proud human beings of African descent.

But keep in mind, this is nothing new. I am not necessarily saying something that has never popped up in discussion, or maybe is has not? I do not know; am I preaching or am I teaching?

Also, think about when parents would tell their sons, "you're a black man in America, you have to work twice as harder than everyone else." That right there is the sure way of sending your son off to prison. Right off the bat, a parent is telling their son, he is not good enough, because he is "black." Let me not forget about the doll test; look that up. Now because African Americans are portrayed that way on television shows, movies, music, and the news; it has been an unbearable challenge for African American people to survive in the United States of America. It is a challenge, every day for us to survive. Why do you think that when "white" people walk around with loaded guns, chances are more than likely, they will come to no harm? Because other "white" people and police officers are already programmed in their brains to see themselves as, "*innocent; pure; without malice, and harmless.*" Even if they are fully strapped and armed to the teeth.

Also, that police officer does not know who that "white" person could be related to. If he were to shoot and kill a young or middle-aged "white" person, and that person was related to someone very powerful; trust and believe, that police officer will never hear the end of it. That police officer would be thrown under the prison. That young "white" kid's life is too valuable to be gunned down, too many opportunities in society, and those "white and black" police officers know that. For white officers, it would be like shooting their own kids. My God, I remember seeing a video of a "white" person, spitting on a police officer, and that police officer did absolutely nothing; spit? Let that same person be "black;" the only thing he or she would be spitting, is the blood they are spitting up, from the multiple gunshot wounds that the "white" officer would let off.

When a "white" person walks into a store, a restaurant, or any establishment for that matter; the worker of that establishment will not be on alert, fearing for their life. They feel that they are in good and "*pure*" company. In that worker's mind, they are consciously aware that this "white" person means no harm to them, because by definition, "whiteness" is harmless.

But let the tables turn and there arrives a "black" person. That same worker could be looking at the "black" person, keeping their eyes on them, making sure they do not steal something out of that establishment. Looking at the surveillance cameras every step of the way.

This is nothing new; that is what makes this "black and white" pandemic, this dilemma, such a toxic atmosphere in the American society. So, when you hear the term, "white supremacy," that is a standard that some people are trying desperately to live by. Some, not all Caucasian people. But the truth is, even though some Caucasian people are not pushing the "white supremacy" agenda, as a whole, it benefits the entire Caucasian population. Which is why I do have much respect for those, who are Caucasian, who have been standing up for what they believe in. For going against the social injustices of our lifetime. I say thank you to them, for their moral values, their integrity, and their sanity.

With all of this being said, my whole point with where I stand; this war between black and white must die, before it kills us all. The stereotypes and stigmas of black and white are the bane of our existence, and we have to put an end to it.

Again, I understand that there is too much history with "black and white," but it is destroying us, no one is benefitting, especially African Americans. I understand that many African American people will not agree with me on this, and I say to them, "do not blacklist me." Do not have me cancelled, because once again, those definitions of the word "black" does not define me as a person, nor should they define you. Also, let me just say this; in no way is my attitude behind or beneath what I am saying, the same attitude that O.J. Simpson had, back when he made his famous statement, "*I'm not black, I'm O.J.*"

That is absolutely not my intentions in what I am discussing right here. Again, I am very proud to be a man of African descent. I am not trying to remove or isolate myself away from the African American community. I am just no longer using the perception of "black" to define our existence on this earth. We are not evil, wicked people. I see us better off without that cursed and toxic identification. Just so I make myself perfectly clear. I hope I have made myself clear.

When it comes to all of this "black and white," I am incredibly sick and tired of it all. Look at it now with the whole "Black Lives Matter" symbol. People have stolen it from the African American community and are now using that as a coupon for their own agendas. Corporations are capitalizing and profiting on it every day. I believe it to be a complete tragedy, in this nation we call America, that in order to contain the insanity of people's killer instant, that you have to put up banners and mark public streets and basketball courts, just to give people a heads up that our lives matter.

It is unbelievably insane that we as African Americans have to live in a society that has to put up banners or mark public places, just to inform the non-African Americans to not harm us or take our lives. What kind of country is that to live in or to be proud of?

It is like America has become this huge rap album, and the "Black Lives Matter" symbol has become the "*Parental Advisory Explicit Lyrics*" label. It has become this warning symbol for people. All of a sudden we now have to remind others that our lives matter? We as African Americans should not have to remind people that our lives matter. That is absolutely ridiculous, and an insult to our existence. After all our history in building this country, our history in inventions, our history in science, mathematics, music, sports, leadership, and also, being elected as President of the United States of America; twice.

Our value, our worth as human beings should not have to be a notification on people's phones, or an advertisement. People need to ask questions; why are there people in America who wants to kill so badly? What are people gaining by taking a life? That evil man who took George Floyd's life, what does he gain from making a man suffer for eight minutes and forty-six seconds? What does that evil man gain from shooting Jacob Blake in the back seven times, in front of Blake's kids? What did Zimmerman gain from killing Trayvon Martin? What did they all gain? The list goes on and on, I cannot even list all of the killings. What are all these killings for? For "white supremacy?"

What is it all for, what are these individuals gaining from taking a life? Shooting and killing people; for what? Something within me says that maybe, just maybe, I should not fault the occupation of law enforcement, over faulting the actual people who kills unarmed African American people. You may need me to elaborate on that a little more, right?

Okay, so what I mean is, we tend to put the blame on police departments, for why African American people are being killed. However, I do not believe that we should blame entirely, the police departments, before we hold the actual men or women police officers responsible. For it is their individual choice to draw their guns and excessively open fire on unarmed African Americans. It is their piss poor judgment that makes law enforcement, generally speaking, look unprofessional, psychotic, and inhumane. I would say definitely, police departments have to reconstruct their training regiment, and who they hire. I do not want people to think that there are no good cops out there, or none left. I truly believe there are.

But as I was saying before, hundreds of thousands of years of human evolution has been tragically reduced to "black and white." Think about it; there are Asian, Latino, Middle Eastern, Indian, and we call ourselves "black and white." We are not colors! Yes, we have different complexions, but to identify ourselves as a color? We will not survive if we do not put an end to this.

To add to that; think about how many children are out there, who are mixed with "black and white." Throughout their whole life, they had to contemplate with their identity. Are they black? Are they white? They love both parents, but the pressure of society is on them to choose which side they are on. Think about how many are out there, stuck in cultural limbo, not knowing which side to choose, which then eventually turns into them not knowing themselves or loving themselves. Not able to live up to anyone's standards, and then they eventually self-destruct. It begins at the early stages of childhood; They self-destruct with drugs, alcohol, become rebellious, then they become lost and an outcast. All because they are of mixed cultures and society compels them to choose a side. When all they really have to do is be human. They become the middle child to society. A middle child to the war of "black and white."

Here is the thing; I cannot and will not tell anyone how they should identify themselves. I can only speak for myself, and from now on, I identify only as an African American, or as a man of African descent. I carry myself without those negative definitions of the word "black." You can do your research on this and see for yourselves.

One more thing, I am not saying that because of our history, that Caucasian people; Europeans, should not be proud of who they are. I am not putting that energy out there at all. I have respect for people from all different walks of life, different ethnicities, nationalities, male, female, and non-binary. There is nothing wrong with being a Caucasian person; I have met, love and respect a great deal of Caucasian people. It is just now I will say, "I won't call you white if you do not call me black." That is my way of thinking. By changing our thinking, we change our behavior, and by changing our behavior, we change the world.

Be proud of who you are, be alive. That is another thing too. I know you have heard this saying over and over again, "life's too short," right? Forgive me; but to me, that phrase is so negative and unappreciative. I mean, if you live long enough, like in your eighties, I am sure you would not say, "life is short." I am sure, someone who is doing life in prison, they would say that life is not as short, but rather long. Now yes, life can be cut short, but you still have to appreciate the time you are blessed with while you are here. Life is not this punishment, nor is death. Do not drown yourself in misery just because the world shows you the worse of it at times. Instead of saying, "life's too short," when people are feeling down, tell them, "you're too alive" to be feeling down. We are too alive to be letting the nonsense and bullshit bring us down. (I tried my best to not include too much cussing in my books, please forgive me).

But yes, you are too alive to be letting people get the best of you or upsetting you because of some disagreements. You are too alive to be afraid of change. Remove the phrase, "life's too short" from your thoughts. Replace it with, "You're too alive." The next time you have a breakup and your heartbroken, say to yourself, "I'm too alive to not move on with my life and meet someone else." The next time you are dealing with bills or going through depression, say to yourself, "I'm too alive to be stressing over temporary issues."

You are too alive today, to worry about things you possibly cannot control. Remember, do not live your life to please and seek validation from random strangers that you will never even know. I spoke about that in my first book, "*Logged Off: My Journey of Escaping the Social Media World*." You are too alive for chasing acceptance. Respect is all you shall ever wish. I believe that the reason why so many people fall into a deep depression, is because they are trying desperately to live up to the expectations of other people, and when they fail those people, they ultimately fail themselves. When people try to live up to how other people define them, they lose themselves, and by losing themselves, they lose hope, and they lose faith. I believe people's greatest fear is being a loser. I truly believe that is why some, not all, but some Caucasian people try so desperately to live up to this whole "white" agenda. This idea of being pure, innocent, and supreme. But when they fail, violence breaks out.

The whole "white supremacy" has become this poisonous, crippling standard. This expectation that was stamped on this land by their founding fathers. Which is why so many individuals are trying to hold on to this for dear life, because if they lose it, there's no going back. I believe that is why we have seen more and more mass and school shootings in America, by the hands of individual Caucasian people, within the last several years. I believe "white supremacy" is a crippling, toxic standard that has been force feed and programmed into the minds of many generations of Caucasian people. It is this vision of preordained greatness, that was achieved through a very inhumane legacy.

Fortunately, many are not trying to participate or live up to this standard. Many are respectfully waking up and fighting against white supremacy. But let me be very clear, there were many great Caucasian men and women who have existed. Shakespeare, Steve Jobs, Walt Disney, Albert Einstein, Frank Sinatra, Hedy Lamarr; just to name several. Those who created computers and a new wave of technology. I do not ignore the innovators. There is nothing wrong with being great or striving for greatness. But remember this; it is never worth being great, if it brings out the worst in you, or if others are left worse off. Perhaps that is something that Trump never heard before or thought about.

However, these are just my thoughts, my opinions, and trust me; I have proofread this section multiple times, and I stand by what I believe, how I feel, and I will keep the same energy about all of what was written. You are more than welcomed to disagree with me. But a lot of people out there, many leaders who do not have any answers for the public. My answer is simply; black and white must die, along with this poisonous standard of "white supremacy." I have hope for us; you know why? Because neither groups have ever called themselves, "black perfection" or "white perfection." You may have heard the terms "white privilege," and "white supremacy," but you will never hear "white perfection." That is what gives me hope. We all know, that none of us are perfect. We are simply these imperfect human beings.

We must once and for all see and respect ourselves as people, as human beings, and not as these divided people of colors. I know many people will always identify as black and white, for the rest of their lives. I do not expect grown adults to change their way of thinking now. But for the youth, hopefully you will be the chosen ones. Hopefully it will be you who take this message and carry it onto your legacies. I do not expect this to happen in our lifetime, in the year 2020. We are extremely divided right now. But I train the muscle of hope, every day. I train it, I dream of it, and I believe it will be possible. To live in a world where we are not "black and white" anymore. A world where we are brothers and sisters who have saved ourselves from self-destruction. We are too alive to say it is too late.

Teachers (08/29/20 10:00 PM)

Waking up to a new day, buzzing alarm,
Out of bed, the stretching, the yawns.
Shower, get dress, coffee, going to be late,
Heading to class; good morning, good morning, lesson plans to create.
A flock of students arrive, class is in session,
Good morning class, here is today's lesson.
Class has started, late students come without a pen or book,
Begging the teachers to let them off the hook.
Teachers full of answers, but students empty of questions,
So full, teachers begin to suffer indigestion.
The stress to teach, dress codes not reached,
Markers and erasers, no more chalkboard screech.
Multiple periods, multiple bells,
Students dropping out, students expelled.
Students cutting classes, bathroom pass to run the hallways,
Day in and day out, thank God it's Friday.
Not enough paper, can't print, broken machines,
Another alternative, PowerPoint presentations on the projector screens.
Teachers asking for homework, every excuse in the book,
Once again, students begging to be let off the hook.
Teacher's lounge; all the stress and tears,

They love them all but can't save them all is what teachers fear.
Politics; parents sending teachers rude emails,
Asking teachers if their child can still pass the class, a hundred absences; they're living a fairytale.
The most important profession in the world, unappreciated and ignored,
The disrespect of telling a teacher, "when I'm in your class, I'm so bored.
Decades of their lives, hoped they made a difference,
Hoped they sparked young minds, drawn some interest.
Now there's virtual learning; digital class is in session,
Students can't log in from home, lost Wi-Fi signal, poor connection.
Can't tell if students are being honest or if it's a bluff,
Nationwide resignations, teachers have had enough.
How could their dream job become a nightmare,
Teachers speaking at board meetings, but do they care?
Hundreds of kids in their classes, and kids of their own,
Spending hours a day with kids at school, barley have time for their kids at home.
Teachers; papers, numbers and grades,
Bills are always coming, paychecks delayed.
How many answers have you left blank?
How many teachers have you ever thanked?

Sunday Service (Sun. 08/30/20 12:24 PM)

Dear God, I thank you for the blessing of life before we die,
Your creativity is of no other; billowy clouds in the sky.
Birds flying oh so high, levitated life with echoey chirps,
The precious moments of baby births and burps.
Your answered prayers come in everlasting layers,
I pray that my that life goes on, hair becomes grayer.
I thank you for today, no promises of tomorrow,
Your forgiveness is miraculous, billions reveal their sorrow.
Your intuition of our ambitions; our dreams we pursue,
Our pursuit of happiness; you make our dreams come true.
The devil comes, the devil goes; he can't buy us all,
Yet you still accept our repentance and catch us before we fall.
We fall to our knees and we pray to you,
You listen to everything that we say to you.
Forgive me, forgive us for our petitioned prayers for the things we can't afford,
Nothing is free in this world, except for the Lord.
Too many questions of why, with very little of "thanks,"
Forgive us for the nuclear bombs, guns and bullets, and military tanks.
Centuries of wars have been declared and brutally fought,
Centuries of slavery, and yet racism is still being taught.

Forgive us for our ignorance; without you, many are lost,
The devil wants our souls, doesn't matter the cost.
He won't get mines, that I will assure,
I'm protected by your blessing, because of you my heart is pure.
I give you all the praises, all the love, and all the credit,
I knew when I gave my life to you, I would never regret it.
I thank you for my family, and my true friends,
My you continue to watch over them all until the very end.
Many names; God, Allah, Buddha, Jehovah,
All praises to the highest; hallelujah.
I thank you for releasing us from the barracoons, yet many are still not free,
Many are mentally enslaved by fortune, fame, and the corporate powers that be.
Amen, amen; all I can say is Amen,
My sacred soul, I shall protect within.
My God, thank you for this gift to write,
Thank you for the many birthdays, and many good nights.
I pray for many more, I pray that is your plan,
I thank you for my mother, for raising me to be a great man.
In my thirties now; a whole new chapter,
The best is yet to come, the best I have yet to capture.
Amen, amen; I look in the sky and say amen,
To my loved ones in heaven; I love you; until we meet again.

Happiness (08/30/20 1:00 PM)

Paid bills, no looting or unsolicited kills,
No black and white, beautiful days and nights,
No arguments or grudges, peace is in everyone's budget,
Mental and physical health, education creates generational wealth.
Hugs and kisses; understanding what bliss is,
Equality; she cooks the meals and you do the dishes.
Vice versa if he's the better cook,
Knowledge is power; interest is the key to crack open a book.
Standing or laying on the sandy bed of the earth,
The sounds of ocean waves, God's design of mirth.
Give birth to your happiness, experience this thing called life,
Feel the wind hug your body; an invisible blanket to cover you at the birth of a new night.
To love and to know the truth, no room for hate and lies,
Tears of happiness when joy comes to you, and the pain dies.
Happiness; to not have much, and to be happy is the goal,
To give more than you receive; it sooths the soul.
I don't need much, all I ask for is today, and hopefully tomorrow,
You're too alive to stress over money and items, just thank God for the time borrowed.
Get some rest, dismiss the burdens and stress,

Your opened eyes; congratulations, you have another day of happiness.

A Date to Remember (08/30/20 6:38 PM)

Wet footprints of four feet decorates the sand,
Two bodies walking side by side, locked hands.
Two strangers slowly becoming lovers,
They're so in sync, can't keep their hands off each other.
The sun slowly sinking down the horizon, a sunset to remember,
They hold each other as they watch the sky linger in amber.
He looks in her eyes and says, "thank you for giving me a second chance,"
She responded, "everyone deserves a second chance," as she looked with a forgiving glance.
They had their problems, but the past will no longer last,
If this were a movie, they make a beautiful cast.
What a hug; he plants his face in the ocean scented layers of her hair,
A burst of laughter as they have an awkward stare.
He looks for two seashells; one for her, one for him,
The sun has abandoned them, too much night to swim.
Finally, he finds two in the sand,
He gives her the big one, it's as big as her hand.
He said to her, "this clam is my heart, and you are the pearl,"
From this day forth, you are my number one girl."
A teary-eyed glare as she looks up at his face,

She knows now, that no other woman will ever take her place.
He lifts her up like a baby, twirls her around in the wind,
She closed her eyes, all her doubts shall die, this is her future husband.
True love; a night when two shall become one,
A date to remember; arise the morning sun.

Electronic Birds (08/31/20 8:28 PM)

The sky full of levitating transport,
Multiple takeoffs, where's the nearest airport?
I wonder where in the world are they going?
London, Tokyo, Paris, I have no way of knowing.
Perhaps they are escaping, moving to start another life,
A couple on their honeymoon, husband and wife.
The flickering lights in the night sky,
Like little flying pebbles miles high.
Always a blessing when they safely land,
Traveling all over the world, people arriving to a foreign land.
Some love to fly, some are petrified,
Humans really can fly, as long as it's electrified.
Hundreds of passengers, going their separate ways,
Good days, bad days, punctual takeoffs, hourly delays.
Once in a lifetime views, city lights from above,
Long distance relationships; getting off the plane to finally meet their true love.
Keep traveling like you've never traveled before,
The world is worth seeing, you're too alive, continue to explore.

"One day; If we, African Americans, no longer identify with "black," we will destroy their power of insult."

Alone with Mariah (08/31/20 9:44 PM)

Crystal clear night, sitting on my deck,
head laying on my pillow, tilted neck.
Lonely with LEDs, candles, and the cadence of crickets,
Then I turned on Mariah; my God, it's like I have front row tickets.
Her voice is of heaven's breath,
I could just cry until there is not a tear left.
The healing her voice harmonically brings,
I thank God she was born; born to sing.
Listening to her on this chilly night,
No pain, no heartbreak, not a worry in sight.
Her melodies; running through my body, mind, and spirit,
Doesn't matter the song; her voice, I just want to hear it.
Her high notes, reaching the farthest end of the universe,
Never heard anything like it; a blessing, or a curse?
My ears are her biggest fans, so many songs,
Hit after hit, she never disappoints, can't go wrong.
A voice that can cure heartache, clear your mental scars,
God I could melt when she hits that last note in
"Never Too Far."
The voice of an angel captured on record forever,
Thinking to myself, "there is never going to be another like her, never."

Her voice gives me peace, I dismiss my sorrow,
I could listen to *Butterfly* from now to tomorrow.

Dear God, thank you for this enchanted fairy,

Thank you for the creation of Mariah Carey.

Throwback Heartbreak

Since we were kids playing on the seesaw,

You showed me your manipulation and your flaws.

Blackmailed me like, "Imma tell your momma, she'll spank you,"

Asked me for my last candy, but can I get a thank you?

Just a little girl in your own princess world,

You had me wrapped around your finger, twisted and twirled.

You were my very first kiss,

Another boy came around; now I'm the boy you dissed.

Played with me like a jump rope,

Every time I tried to sweep you off your feet, you jumped, it was no hope.

Teenagers now, you ignored me because I put on some weight,

I wasn't cool enough, wouldn't talk to me, we were even classmates.

I lost the weight, but you couldn't wait to play me again,

I made you smile, but he made you laugh, a step ahead in the game.

I just couldn't win with you, heartbreak since five,

Toys in our cubby, didn't like show and tell, I was too shy.

I feared I spoiled you to hurt me,

You take pleasure in leading me on, just to desert me.

I learned many lessons, it’s a blessing we’re apart,

Keeping my distance from you, you’re a plague to my heart.

Not kids anymore, we’re grown,

Keep your hellos and goodbyes, no thank you to your friend zone.

I forgive but never forget,

I’m healed with no regrets.

Thanks to Hov (09/4/20 2:42 PM)

Graduated from college, sweat from debt,
Future wasn't set, but I gained the knowledge.
I don't see 9 to 5 in my mentality,
Millionaire is more of a reality.

Maybe a billion more, that comes with corporate drama,
More commas, looking like banana pajamas,
Making money in my sleep, wrapped in sheets,
Like the Dalai Lama.

Living in boxes like a checkerboard,
But I played chess, never under arrest,
I wrote my blessing, pen mightier than the sword.

Make money to afford but not to buy the wants and needs,
"I Want You" American dream like Apollo Creed,
Never touched the weed, seduced by the greed,
Stop posting and read,
Get some pages and bleed.

I can't wait, no more chasing a date,
Kept my fate, built my empire,
Now I open and close my own gates.

I'm chasing wealth with good health,
Cards dealt, pain felt, but in the end, I have that
championship belt.

Laughed at my book dreams, then
my book reached
top 25 on Amazon kindle streams.

I take words and make poetic soup,
To feed the poorly educated groups,
I went from baggy jeans to Italian suits,
Sadly teens, I see them loot, shoot,
Buried and became roots before they knew their roots.

Friends they're going to come and go,
Favors will be running slow,
Then they come back when you're about to blow,
Your real friends are the ones who stick around
after you tell them "no."

Hood filled with potential that's never reached,
More gun shots than jump shots, drive-by screech,
Don't hate your complexion, get rid of the bleach,
Kids buck-fifty classes; not hearing teachers preach.

Handcuffed hospital beds and ICU,
Throwing us in the concrete forest,
Hit us with that Whitaker sniper like, "Eye see you."
Blind eyes nationwide; detectives don't have a clue?
All of this under the red, white, and blue?

Kaepernick took a knee,
He wants his people to be free,
In the same land where his people were hung from trees,
Enough with these killing sprees,
You're killing me, you're killing thee, you're killing we,
can't you see?

Murder is never something to gain,
You'll still be miserably stuck in this life-long game,
Only victims point fingers to blame,
Help the brain refrain from going insane,
Military trained, showers of bullets, that's police rain,
Police remain not charged; fuck your race card,
Don't call me black no more, put some respect on my name.

Burn Out (08/29/20 11:16 PM)

No more words in my chamber of thoughts,
Blind to my vision, hazy depictions.
My genius has disappeared from my psyche,
The motivation has been dismissed.
I ran out of stories to tell, what more can I say?
Crashing thoughts in a horrible brainstorm,
The thunder of my voice is gone,
The lightning of my thought process is not sparking.
Perhaps I am just in the way,
Blocking my blessings, incarcerating my genius to stay inside my mind.
Numbed to my writing; several books in under a year, I'm so tired.
Pushed my potential far beyond the finish line of greatness.
I won first place of satisfaction,
But first runner up for a completed legacy.
My brain can't wait, it's ready for a vacation,
No written words for the remainder of the year.
No more computer screens glaring in my face,
No more digital files transferring and submitting the work.
Maybe I should cry my happiness out and let it soak back inside of me.
I did my best in a brief period of time,

My mind deserves this break in definitely.

Creative burn out never felt so good.

You know why?

Because it lets you know that you've reached your truest potential, and you have nothing to prove to anyone.

Say congratulations with a pat on the back,

I've done well,

But now I must recharge and do some more healing.

I wrote my pain, my fears, my anger and regrets; I wrote it all.

I released all that I have to you, for now.

This feels good, it feels great. No one can ever take this away from me.

Thank God, he is oh so amazing.

Until next time.

Thank you.

Conclusion

There you have it! I have given you the best that I have, for now. I have given you many of my thoughts, my dreams, my imagination, my pain; and it was my pleasure to share this with you. Wow, this is mind boggling to me. I would not have ever imagined that I would be writing books. I sometimes have to pinch myself to make sure I am not daydreaming. This book, "*The Healing*," is my third book in under eleven months. I literally wrote and published three books in under a year. I find it hard to believe sometimes, but I am glad that it is my reality.

I remember when I was riding somewhere with my mother, and I had my laptop with me. I was just starting to write the introduction to my first book. She looked at me and asked, "what are you writing?" I said, "I'm writing a book." She did not say anything, she just looked at me and laugh. But of course, I did not take no offense to it. That is my mother, she knows me more than anyone.

But I am the type of person, that when I have something in my mind, when I have an idea, a vision, I have to see it through. I stuck with it, I kept writing and writing until I reached the end of my first book. I was so proud that day, when the proof copies of my first book came in the mail. When I opened the package, saw my face and name on the book cover, I was speechless. I could not say a word. I was at a lost for them. Especially considering the fact that I wrote over eighty thousand words in my first book. I was very proud that day, very proud indeed.

I flickered over the pages, looking at my words, thinking to myself, "I can't believe I did this; I cannot believe I wrote a book." From that moment on, I knew that as long as I put my mind to something, and I work hard and stay committed to it, anything is possible. Then, I went ahead and wrote my second book, "*Mirrors and Reflections*." I had the same speechless feeling, and now here we are. You have just read my third book, "*The Healing*." Now I am sure that some of you who are reading this right now, this may be your first time reading my work, this may be the first book you have read of my collection. Well, first let me say thank you for giving it a chance, and no worries; you can always catch up and read the first two books later.

But yes, I am very proud of what I have accomplished within the span of eleven months. I started writing my first book back in October of 2019, and now I have completed my third in September of 2020; God is great. What I will say about all of this; I am filled with immense satisfaction. That is the thing too. When you achieve something, I believe it is very important that you have satisfaction after you have achieved whatever it is that you want to achieve in life.

It is so important; because the very last thing you want to do, is accomplish something, and afterwards you still do not feel complete or satisfied. I feel that a lot of people become misconstrued with the art of satisfaction. People tend to believe that they can be satisfied with materialism. For example, if someone purchases a car, and right after they drive off the lot, right then, the value of that car decreases. They take the car home, probably show it off to family and friends on social media, and then receive likes and comments on their post. Then after a while, those likes and comments fade, and what will happen is that person will think, "*what is the next thing I need to buy*?" The cycle then continues, the cycle of consumption, because materialism casuses unsatisfaction. I do not believe you can achieve satisfaction through buying things, items, or materialistic objects. You will buy one thing, and just want to buy more and more.

Then people begin to go through a hoarding phase, keeping all types of objects in their homes, thinking they will need them, when really they become toxic to their environments. The art of satisfaction, for me, is simply having less things, that brings value to my life. I spoke about these two men before in my first book. Two men by the name of Joshua Fields Millburn and Ryan Nicodemus, who are self-proclaimed Minimalist.

I truly believe their lifestyle has contributed to my mental health and my healing. When I saw their documentary, "*Minimalism: A Documentary About the Important Things*." It changed my way of living and consuming. It changed my life. I learned that it is important to love people and like things; and to not have it be the other way around.

So, with all of that being said, with the art of satisfaction, I have found my satisfaction in writing my books. I have reached my truest potential. Once I put this book out there into the universe, I know that I have served a purpose. A purpose of healing not just myself, but possibly the healing of others. In this year 2020, it has been a year that we just did not see coming. A year of much heartbreak and trauma. As well as stress, and with this up and coming election, we will all be in need of some healing. Some escapism so to speak.

For you, the reader; who loves poetry, who finds escapism through reading, I am glad that you found this book. I am grateful that you saw this book online, or possibly one day in a bookstore; and during this crisis of a pandemic, you chose to spend your hard-earned money on my book. I cannot tell you how much I appreciate you. You could have spent your money on anything else, yet you chose to spend it on this book and support my work.

I am forever grateful to you, wherever you may be; in America, the United Kingdom, Australia, Canada, wherever, I thank you. You are most definitely appreciated. I hope you were able to find some connections, perhaps some of the poetry you may relate to, or possibly have experienced in your actual life.

To be honest with you, a lot of what I wrote, I just laid in my bed, looked up at the ceiling, and the words just came falling down. The visons that I had in my mind were floating in mid-air, and peacefully landed on the runway of my thoughts. Sometimes I had no idea where these visions came from. My best guess, no, I will say they came from above. They came from the spirits, from God, I have to give God that due credit.

As I said earlier, this was not the book I initially had in mind. I was going in a completely different direction. I was in the midst of writing a book about America. I guess you can say that it was going to be a more politically driven narrative, perhaps very controversial. But as I came to the completion of the second chapter, there was something inside of me saying, "stop." There was this energy within me, telling me that this is not the way. This is not the book the world needs right now. The universe did not want me to have it.

So, I no longer pursued it. Even though I felt that I was touching on some very valid points and that it would be a great read; I followed my gut, my intuition, and I took the direction that God wanted me to take. Let me say, I am actually glad I took this route and created another collection of poetry to share with the world.

I felt that the world is in such pain right now. Hundreds of thousands of human beings have lost their lives during these last several months. New Covid-19 cases are coming through on a daily basis, and I realized that no one wants to read a book about America's problems. Hell, the world has problems. So, I am really grateful that I did not pursue the book I originally was writing before I even thought of "*The Healing*."

I am not sure if I will ever go back to that book. But I did save it, for if the universe ever wants me to have it, perhaps I will continue writing. But that will probably be a long ways ahead before I put out another book. Because after writing this one, I have definitely reached creative burn out. I kid you not, I cannot think of anything else to write about at the moment. For the last eleven months, my brain, my eyes, my money, my time, and my commitment has been dedicated to these books. I am sure I have bored my friends and family by now, with all these talks about my books.

Not that they are aggravated; but it has been one book after the other, and it has been difficult for people to keep up. So, I try to avoid speaking about books with my family and friends altogether. But yes, this book kind of left me on empty, I must admit. I said to myself, "once I complete this book, I do not want to touch my laptop for at least a year." I mean just that too, as far writing another book. I will take a brief break.

But I will say that overall, this has been an incredible journey for me. It has been an absolute blessing. To share such personal, somewhat private details of my life. To be open and vulnerable within my writings, to be naked even. To accept the fact that some people will love it, love the work, and there will be some who are not a fan. That is okay for me either way. I know that my style of writing may not be up to certain readers' standards, especially in this new era of what people call, "Insta-poetry."

Since I am no longer on social media, I cannot say that I am an insta-poet, or that I follow the same formula or style of that world. Not that I have anything against it, to each is own. However, I have a very complex way of writing these stories. I would never be satisfied with having only a handful of lines, and that would be the poem. Again, nothing against those who write that way; I have read some when I was on social media, and they were very good.

But I have to go my own way. Even if I do not sell thousands of copies, or millions, I can live and be grateful with the hundreds of you who purchase a copy of my books. I think you guys and gals are terrific.

I will say this, I do not have much of a presence on the internet. I do use it when necessary, of course. However, I found that it does take its toll on many of us, especially in the social media era. If or when you ever have a chance to read my first book, "*Logged Off: My Journey of Escaping the Social Media World*," you will understand why I had to take my leave. It was becoming toxic for me. It became a place of distraction rather than a place of growing and connecting with people. It became a disconnect, a mental health problem.

The reason I brought that up is because when I left all of the social media behind me two years ago, that was the beginning stages of healing. That was the starting point of my healing process, and to be perfectly honest with you, it was the best decision I could have made for myself. I found myself once I logged off. I found God again. My mental health began to increase and stabilize. So, I made the decision to abandon the social media world forever. I abandon my presence on the internet.

One thing I wanted to mention about social media and technology. We have taken the natural ingenious computer that we call our brain, and built these computers outside of our minds, to do the work for us. What this new wave of technology has done, is it has left our minds to be vacant and empty, with no real knowledge, and no logical thinking. First we created computers that stood taller than man, then came the computers on a desk, then a computer on our laps, and now there's the computers in our pockets that we call smartphones. With this new technology, hypothetically speaking, we blew our brains out, into these devices. I believe that is why people are naturally addicted to these products. These products, the smartphones, are brain replacements. Think about it; they capture our greatest memories, they think for us, they talk for us, and we live through them. They own us, as I said before.

It is amazing how what we as people create, gradually becomes our downfall, unintentionally. But do not get me wrong, I appreciate the new wave of technology. Without it, I would not have been able to have these books. So, I respect the innovation of it. However, years from now there could be a generation of empty minded, brain dead stoners. A new wave of mentally enslaved zombies, looking to record anything that bleeds. But anyways, that is food for thought.

I really do not feel the need or desire to be famous. I rather my work be famous than myself. One of the reasons why I deleted all of my accounts. After what we have experienced in the year 2020, I do not even believe in fame anymore. Fame is only for gimmicks. I remember seeing a video of Jimi Hendrix, in the video he said, "*the world is nothing but a big gimmick.*" I am not a gimmick, I am an artist, a man, a human being of African descent. That is my definition of who I am, in this world, and in this life.

I would recommend that for you as well. Find yourself, define yourself, stay true to yourself, and go your own way. Do not worry about having a lot of friends; I said this before and I will say it again in this book, "the greatest friend you will ever have in this life, is tomorrow." You have nothing if you do not have tomorrow. I guarantee you, you take a break from these gadgets and platforms, get to know yourself, you will find the healing that you have been praying for, for so long.

Remember, you are too alive to hold grudges, holding on to the painful past, or whatever issues you had to endure in your life. You are too alive. Look in the mirror every morning and say to yourself, "I'm too alive." It does not cost you anything to love yourself. That is what people will never teach you. We are conditioned to believe that buying things creates our happiness, but to love yourself, that is absolutely free.

But the question you may be asking yourself, "what is the benefit of loving myself?" You may be asking, "what do I get out of loving myself?" You get your mental health, you get good energy, you become wiser, you take care of yourself, and in return, people will sense that good energy from you, and they will want to be around you. You see? You receive all of that, for free, just by loving yourself. That is why when people buy so many things, they still cannot find satisfaction, they cannot find themselves. They become lost and enslaved in the world of consumption.

So, in these final thoughts, I would like to ask you this one thing. "What is healing for you?" What must you experience in reality, to grow and mature, and to find healing? Do you seek therapy? Do you have mentors that you talk to? Do you pray and talk to God? I know this is a silly question, but do you talk to yourself? Do you have many thoughts, so many, that you just have to speak them out loud, in a room by yourself?

There are no judgments, we are all different and we handle things differently. We morn differently, respond differently, and it is okay. Healing is a process; I do not expect anyone to read this book, and suddenly overnight they are healed. Healing is a process; it is a good process to have. But I must say this as well; there can never be healing without the truth.

You can drown yourself in an ocean of lies. Only the truth can bring you to the surface. The healing process is you learning how to swim; metaphorically speaking of course. By now you should know that I am a heavily philosophical thinker. But yes, without the truth, you cannot find healing. I had to tell my truth in my first book in order to truly seek the healing that I needed, and let me tell you, it was worthwhile. I gave up the façade and became my authentic self. It took much work, but I am healing for sure.

But anyways, I hope you, the reader, enjoyed this journey I put you through. If you have been around since the first book; your love and support mean everything to me. Considering the fact that I had no idea that I would be a published author. You have supported all of my work. I cannot thank you enough, you are amazing. As for you newcomers, I appreciate you very much. You took a chance on an unknown man. If you love my work, there is much more where that came from.

I would also like to say this, and then I will conclude this journey. I wanted to save this for the very end. It is a question. Whether you are in bed at the moment of reading this particular part, or outside somewhere, does not matter the time. If you can, please answer this question. The question is, "*Think about your loved ones who have passed away. If you could bring one back, that could give you healing, who would that be*? You do not have to reveal the answer to anyone. But I do ask, if you have anything to say to this loved one, write it down on a piece of paper, and keep it to yourself. You can write something brief, a poem, love note, whatever you feel would give you some closure or healing. I would not suggest posting it. Really try to keep it for yourself. But if there is anything you want to say to that loved one, but did not have the chance to say it, now is your chance.

Just because they are no longer here with us, in the physical form, that does not mean you have to let them go from your mind or your heart. I think you know that already. Writing is therapeutic, write what you feel. I know; It is quite difficult, isn't it? We all have more than one person, who has passed away, that we would love to bring back, and talk to. It is a very difficult question; I struggled answering this myself.

But that is all for now. Once again, I cannot thank you all enough, for making it this far. I hope through some of these stories, you experienced some entertainment, connections, forgiveness for people in your personal life, and possibly, some healing. Remember, healing is a process, and any kind of processing takes time. "*The pain will win some battles, but love will always win the war.*"

For those of you reading this in the year 2020; please stay safe. I pray we survive this strange metamorphosis and remember; you are too alive. Take care of yourself and others. God bless you; until next time.

Thank You

First and foremost, I have to thank God for the blessing. Without God, none of this would have been possible. God most definitely guided me through, not just this book, but all three of them. Next I would like to thank you, the reader, for your time. I know poetry is not the easiest thing to read and understand. So, poetry readers always take a chance. I thank you all very much for the love and support. It means so much, it is a very big deal for me.

Of course, I thank my mother and father for bringing me into this world. I thank, once again, my High School African American history teacher, Ms. Rich, for her spark of inspiration for me to start writing poetry. I thank my former college professor Henry "Hank" Stewart again, for helping me with my writing craft. I also want to thank the few friends I have, and my family for all the love and support.

Lastly, I would like to thank those who are not even born yet. I thank you, the future readers, who will one day come across this book, read it, and it just may change your life. You may see your life through this poetry, and you may be inspired to become a writer, a poet. I thank you, the future readers, whether that is five, ten, twenty, or even a hundred years from now. I thank you guys in advance.

With all of that being said, I think we are finished with "*The Healing*." I thank you all, I appreciate you, stay blessed, and until next time. Remember, you are too alive, enjoy your life to the very fullest. Plant your truest potential and watch it grow into greatness. Thanks again and take care.

ABOUT THE AUTHOR

JORDAN WELLS was born and raised in East Orange, New Jersey. He graduated from Centenary University; earning a bachelor's degree in business, with concentrations in finance and marketing. He is also a professional actor, a member of the Screen Actors Guild-American Federation of Television and Radio Artists. "*The Healing*," is Wells' third book. "*Mirrors and Reflections*" is Wells' sophomore book, his debut book, "*Logged Off: My Journey of Escaping the Social Media World*," was a monumental achievement in Wells' life, and will continue on with his creative writing ventures.